WOO DAT!

BRINGING BACK THE OLD
SCHOOL WAY OF WOOING INTO
21ST CENTURY RELATIONSHIPS

Amy Venezia

**Woo Dat! Bringing Back the Old School Way
of Wooing into 21st Century Relationships**

By Amy Venezia
© 2012, All Rights Reserved
www.facebook.com/woodat.me

Cover design:
Hayden Miethe for Misfit Me Creative
Book design:
Sue Balcer of JustYourType.biz

French Quarter Press
Published by FQP

*This book is dedicated to
the man I wish had wooed me
and to the city that did.*

Contents

preface: • vii

one: **Art of the Woo** • 1

two: **Chapter 2: Woo Worthy** • 25

Chapter 3: **Beware of WOOves in Sheep's Clothing** • 47

Chapter 4: **The Master Dater vs. The Master Baiter** • 63

Chapter 5: **Counting Coup** • 77

Chapter 6: **Cafe du Funde'** • 91

Chapter 7: **Woodoo** • 103

Chapter 8: **The Return of the Woo** • 121

Preface

In a way, I could say that this book has been in the making for the last 39 years; certainly it has components of every relationship I have had throughout my life. However, the actual idea for this book came at a time in my life when I had successfully completed a string of relationships. When I say successfully completed, I mean I was very successful at ending all of them.

I first want to make it clear that every single word of this book has come from some experience—or some mistake—that I have made. **I have worn lots of masks there are to wear in relationships.** I was a virgin on the night of my honeymoon. This is the absolute truth. As a result, I went through a stage in my 30's, after a very long relationship, that I probably should have gone through in my college years. After all, I did not have my first alcoholic drink, or even step foot in a club, until I was 25 years old. Maybe that is where some of the insight you will find in this book was gained. I was making choices later in life, with a more mature outlook, and therefore was able to dissect those choices and extract the lessons; something you don't necessarily do in your 20's.

I have been writing about relationships and this human condition we are all a part of for many years. I wrote on these topics as a way of purging. A way for me to release everything my sensitive little being takes in from life and its lessons. But it wasn't until I had experienced something myself, something I had never experienced before, that I finally came to realize what exactly had been missing in my own relationships. It is an odd feeling, being in the generation I am in. We remember simpler times and yet are caught up in this fast-paced world we now live in. Some people bury it in the past. But I have always had this bit of longing in me, a part of me that didn't want to let that simpler life go. I have never wanted to trade in my old school ways of connecting with people for the technological options we have today.

When I look back on my past relationships, I am almost ashamed that I considered them to be love. I am not speaking for the other people in those relationships, I am speaking for me. It wasn't until I had an eye opening experience that I was able to see how I was not stepping up to the plate. I was the player in the dugout that never gets to the plate, yet can still he played the game because he was on the team. There were ways I thrived at love and ways I failed, but regardless, I was always learning. At the end of the day, that's what it's all for anyway: Learning. If you can't embrace that, the hurts and the failures will consume you.

Of course, it wasn't until I got to a place where I was able to lay it all down—the pride and the games and the ego—and say, "Yes! I want to be wooed by this man!" (even though I ended up un-wooed) that I became still enough to realize that the state of my outer experiences were very much a reflection of my own inner world. I needed to clean up, but I wasn't the only one. As I looked around me I saw many people that needed to clean up. By this I mean, we need to be like the person who comes to the door in their Sunday best, a rose in one hand and their heart in the other, willing to be vulnerable. Willing to be real. I mean becoming your best, offering something, and allowing yourself to be fully seen before the person you are pursuing.

My epiphany came in New Orleans. I realized how love and romance are dying arts; how this openness and vulnerability I speak of are avoided like the plague; how we have no one to blame but ourselves. So many people are unhappy, but instead of doing the hard work it takes to change themselves, they have become addicted to technology and the easy way.

Yep, we are an addicted society. Facebook, Twitter, reality shows...these have become our "crack." We are spoon-fed this crack every day, and we all know that crack—please forgive my insensitivity here—is whack! Sorry Whitney...

That said, if you find that you are a little unhappy, a little complacent, a little confused, a little numb, a little indifferent, and if you are ready to change your life, I invite you to read on and take the WOO DAT CHALLENGE!

* ● *

one
The Art of the Woo

"As for me, to love you alone, to make you happy, to do nothing which would contradict your wishes, this is my destiny and the meaning of my life."

— Napoleon Bonaparte

Have you ever seen the Will Smith movie, Hitch? If so, you probably remember the flashback showing how Hitch came to be a professional dating consultant. In the flashback he was so naive, so innocent, as he tried to understand why the girl he had been "in love" with was making-out with another dude in a car. As tears stream down his cheeks in the pouring rain, he bangs on the passenger window, pleading, "Why??". The guy making-out with his girl basically tells him that it's because of what Hitch was doing right then.

We've all been there. Well, most of us have. I definitely have. There are two types in this world: The "Hitches" and the ones making out in the car, not caring a thing about the Hitches. In other words, the wooers and the ones who get wooed. In the dating world today, you are either the one who is too into the person or they are too into you...unless you hit that magical jackpot of love where a relationship actually develops out of a mutual "I'm really into you" feeling. Even in committed relationships, most times there is one that gives and invests more and one that takes and gives less.

Because of this seeming failure to connect and make it last, the art of wooing has been on the endangered list for some time. Intimacy in general suffers because of this; in fact, if we had a National Geographic for relationships, we would have images of malnourished connections all over the place. It is the major missing element from communicating and relating in the world today. It is also the antidote to the stagnant and complacent tendencies we have around commitment.

Imagine all the new connections that might have taken off had it not been for the lack of woo. Imagine all the people who might still be together today.

It is common sense that when you are making the effort to woo you are more selective. This is because wooing takes time, and creativity, and who wants to make that kind of effort for something that means nothing to them? We are all too busy on Facebook for that! You can look at it like the Bachelor/Bachelorette series. It's as if you are down to only one rose, but instead of just two people there is a room full. Knowing you have only one rose and lots of options to choose from, you will be more selective. You will take your time deciding. You will really hone in on the things you are truly seeking in a person. And hopefully, with all of these things combined, your choice will hold some weight.

What exactly is the definition of woo, you might be asking? There are a few definitions out there, but I like this one the best: to solicit or entreat especially with importunity.

To woo is to be intentional about what it is you want to receive. Let's get that straight right now. Wooing is done purposefully, and to receive a desired outcome. Not just for the heck of it. But that's what makes it so great! I was once told that the only way to have a successful transaction with a person (and this was on a business level) was to make sure that each person equally gave and benefited from the transaction. Not one person giving and the other taking. Not one person doing things pro bono for the other's benefit (unless that is the mutual agreement going in that makes both parties happy). A successful transaction means an equal effort and an equal benefit for everyone involved. Why would it be any different for a romantic relationship?

Some might say that is manipulative, even calculated. No, it just means you're smart, savvy, and aware that love is a two-way street. The biggest mistake people make is to take on the belief that love should not take work. Where in the world did we get that belief from? I compare it to work here for this reason: what about those people lucky enough to actually do something they love for a living? They don't feel like it is work. They are excited every day to get up and go to it. It should feel the same with love. If it doesn't, you need to take a deeper look at your relationship. The bottom line is: people are lazy when it comes to relationships. Truly. You see it everywhere. Who and what is to blame for that? Is it the endorphins that stop being produced as frequently once you are with a person for an extended period of time? Do we all of have a case of the "new car smell syndrome", where once we sit in it long enough we no longer notice it until we leave it for some time and come back to it? Is it simply human nature to get bored easily and therefore lose the desire to make an extra effort or any effort at all? Like kids in a playroom letting that toy sit in the corner because we are moving on to the new one? Or, is it like the new car that when you first got you kept shiny and clean at every opportunity... yet as time moves on...the car washes become less and less frequent.

Despite this analogy, I am not saying love is a game or calculated. I am saying that love is like the old saying, "Anything worth having is worth working for." That is where we have gone off-track as a society. If there was a Magellan, an explorer looking for love, he would be hearing, "Make a u-turn at the next possible opportunity" over and over again. Again, somehow

* ● *

we have convinced ourselves that love shouldn't take work. This is especially true of "'80's babies" that think if it takes longer than 60 seconds to get what you want, then on to the next one. Everything worth having in this universe takes effort, so what makes us think that love is any different? Like everything else, it must be nurtured and nourished. Like anything else, no one else is going to come along and do it for you.

While I was visiting New Orleans, I had an epiphany about my past relationships and what they had been missing. Before this trip I hadn't been able to quite put my finger on the missing element. There were the obvious complaints such as, " Well, it would have worked out if he hadn't put me in more awkward positions than the Kama Sutra when it came to cheating, trust, loyalty, or hey! even--just emotional availability." Then there were my obvious shortcomings. But I couldn't narrow it down to one thing...that one key ingredient missing from my happily-ever-after recipe. The ingredient that goes so much deeper than two people trying to combine their lives and never hurting each other for the sake of being ...human. Meaning the tight rope walk we all do in relationships because it seems the average "relationship" is not a safe ground for showing your true self, imperfections and all. Most of us have to strive for perfection or at least the appearance of it for fear of disappointing and losing the other person. "Come on" I thought "there has to be something more." In New Orleans I found it.

I was sitting in the Napoleon House with the co-writer of a screenplay I was working on at the time. My co-writer is an older man--used to more old school ways of courting a person--and he was telling me about how he pursues a woman he is truly interested in. We were speaking of how men from younger generations have not been taught to woo. How women these days wouldn't even know how to receive wooing. I listened to him speak of things that would definitely be considered going the "extra mile." Things that took caring, effort and time. Things that would be considered the old-school way. He was sharing how he had been taught to court a woman. He used the word "woo." I think his exact words were, "Amy, you and every other woman deserve to be wooed." And I replied, in complete enthusiastic agreement, "Yeah! Woo Dat!" and that is when it hit me: This world has lost the way of wooing. It is extinct. A dead art form.

The only thing we need to do is look at the arts, music, and the state of marriage and relations these days for the proof that woo is through.

Most Top 40 music is about partying and hooking up. Reality shows have taken over TV. We live in a youth- obsessed society where perfect bodies and attainment of perfect things is priority number one. Connecting with other people is for fun and thrills. The moment conflict or anything other than pleasure shows itself in the equation, people bail. If it isn't easy, it's not worth it; not when there are so many other options out there. In the dating realm, it is completely normal and almost expected that if someone you meet wants to ask you out, they can do it in a text, not a phone call. It's all about instant gratification, not about actually cultivating a connection with another person.

While enjoying the cheese plate at Napoleon House, I listened to this wise man speak of what many today would consider grandiose gestures. Ever notice how the term "stalker" has become a household word? If anyone makes an effort, goes the extra mile, whether it's writing a letter or sending some flowers, they are stalkers or creepy. If they are persistent, they are stalkers. In the ego-driven society of today, being able to claim a stalker and having many little "stalkers" is as impressive as having the latest iPhone. It's another way to set yourself above and apart, a defense mechanism to keep from having to feel any form of emotion other than superiority.

Think of the great love stories in history; they would all be considered stalker tales today. That man standing outside your window, calling out to you? Stalker. That girl, falling at your feet, wiping her tears with her hair? Stalker. Rumi, one of the greatest poets of all time, wrote of his love for Shams in the most beautiful and eloquent ways. Even after Shams disappears, never to be seen or heard from again, even though they had only known each other for a total of two years, Rumi wrote a lifetime about him. Rumi would be considered a stalker today. Out walking after midnight? You're a stalker. How about if a person you respected or cared about abruptly disappears from the relationship because they are too weak to say it straight? If you want closure and pursue the conversation to get it, you're a stalker. If you don't back down or let go when someone is making a cowardly exit from a connection, you are a stalker.

The whole world is addicted to crazy. He's crazy. She's crazy. I can't say that, he'll think I'm crazy. I can't do that, she'll think I'm crazy. These days, caring equals crazy. "Crazy" has become the 21st century armor, the universal defense mechanism. No one questions crazy. Everyone believes it when they hear it. It is accepted in more places than Visa and MasterCard.

"Whatever happened with that girl?" "She was crazy."

Conversation dropped, along with any accountability in the matter.

"Why aren't you into that guy anymore?" "He was crazy." "Really?? Like how??" "He texted all the time and told me he cared about me like after the third time I hung out with him."

Wow....that's like...crazy.

The truth of the matter is, no one is crazy. Unless

they are going around physically harming people or locking themselves in a room saying, "Come in with the milk." (Who remembers that movie scene?)

So who is going to make the effort to woo when there is a good chance they will be slapped with the crazy label?

Not many.

Why do people do this? Because they don't want to risk the chance of being vulnerable.

Nowadays, most people believe that love is not worth the risk of a broken heart. But that is the problem, for the only way to remove the vulnerability is to remove the heart. Without the heart, there can be no heartbreak. And so they immerse themselves in every distraction possible to keep from feeling something that makes them feel weak and vulnerable. Cue collecting stalkers, social media, TV, partying, calling people crazy, text messaging, Angry Birds...ok... maybe not Angry Birds.

No one wants to jump anymore. Why would they? There are too many people to hook up with on the cliff. Love at first sight is not only unheard of today; it has become a type of stigma. One that, if ever slipped from one's lips, automatically marks them in the "crazy" category. Caring is crazy. Being real is crazy. About the only thing considered sane today is to have little to no emotions.

So is it any surprise that wooing is on life support?

Wooing equals caring. It means caring when

you say no; caring when you say yes; deliberately making a commitment that you don't run from. It means sacrifice over the easy way out. It means your word holds weight, not because you go against what it is you want to do, but because you actually know yourself well enough to know what you want to do. Think about that one! It means having some character. It means having feelings. Not irrational emotional roller coaster feelings, but rather heartfelt feelings.

Despite the current war on love and emotions, there remains a very beautiful truth: You never know what you have until it is gone. Most people are realizing that in this technologically dependent world we are living in, there is something missing. Something so simple and beautiful, the heart of things. Another revelation is that having character and keeping your word when it comes to wooing does not mean the same it did for, let's say, our parents' generation. My parents' generation didn't have a choice. Honor meant doing what you should do, whether you wanted to or not. You just did it. Like today, people back then also shut off their emotions and dreams, because sacrifice was the norm.

Subsequent generations have fought tooth and nail to change that, even if it meant waging war from the couch while playing Xbox. They were going to do what they wanted to do in life. Not stay at some miserable job for 30 years. Not stay in some miserable marriage for life. And so, there was a pendulum swing.

And if you look at how a pendulum swings when you hold it all the way to one side and let go, it swings all the way to its opposite side. Over and over, it goes back and forth until it settles in the middle. We have been to the other extreme for some time now. It is time for it to settle in the middle. It is time for balance. An agreement of sorts, like allies, the heart (feeling) part of us and the logical (technical) part of us joining together for the good of all mankind. Like that old cartoon, which some of you will be too young to remember, used to say, " Wonder powers activate... form of a...." Well, when these two come together you have the form of perfect union within one's self and perfect union is the foundation that will keep a lifetime of woo standing.

It is no longer about morality or rules, but more about choosing what would be the very best for you. Today, we have a choice in the matter. What we build from this time forward can be from something heartfelt and not from a case of the "shoulds." I should do this and I should do that, even though it makes me miserable and goes against everything I really wish I could do. Or a case of the addiction to patterns that we aren't even aware of. Those "types" of people we always seem to go for and always seem to get the same exact results from. We mentioned crazy earlier... Einstein believed that to be the definition,doing the same thing over and over again expecting different results.

* ● *

So, why woo? When you decide to woo in your relationships, you make a commitment to become very clear in your focus and what you are doing to cultivate and nourish that connection. You get to see it grow right before your eyes and the satisfaction that comes from making that choice and making someone else feel so good is worth any effort it takes.

That alone makes wooing cool.

Hardly a day goes by when I don't hear some guy talking about how he doesn't get how girls these days. I too am often shocked by other females. If a man opens a door for a woman, or even holds a door open, there are some women who find this chauvinistic. There are also women, and I have been one of them in the past, that have taken on the trait of chasing, which used to be something "the man" did. There are also women who have chosen the hook-up way of life over the relationship way of life. In the dating and relationship world, people are floundering. The reasons for our epic failure are countless.

Disconnection is one of them.

We live in a disconnected world. Oh, some may say we are the most connected we have ever been. After all, I can be on Facebook and meet someone in Japan--A person I never would have "connected" with in a million years, if not for the wonders of the internet. But this technology-based way of connecting has quickly replaced true connections. It is where our best persona comes out to play, not the real one. We create our little alter ego and set a stage like a reality TV show. We collect our fans, our crazies, and we convince ourselves that who we portray ourselves to be is who we really are. Our heartbeat gets replaced with a techno beat. Now it is all about the party and how good you can feel all the time. And anyone who challenges that gets de-friended and the quest for instant gratification continues.

Couples used to sit across from each other in restaurants, looking each other in the eye and carrying on a conversation; you now have couples sitting, looking at their individual iPhones, waiting for the food to arrive. It used to take time to get to know a person, you now have good ole' Google. Got a name? Type that baby in and go to town judging someone based on what you pull up on the first ten pages. Better yet, run a background check on them. See how they, like everyone else, struggled through the recession. See how many parking tickets they may have or if they have ever gotten arrested for childish shenanigans. You can find out ANYTHING before you even say yes to that coffee invitation.

Think back to the way people used to meet. That time period when they would have to send each other handwritten notes and letters to get to know each other. That time when you couldn't Google and pull up so-and- so's Cancun vacation pictures. Think back to when you met someone and didn't scrutinize them in the first three seconds of that meeting.

Think back to Napoleon's days. That is exactly what I did as I sat in the very house offered to him in 1821 by the mayor of New Orleans, for refuge during his exile. Napoleon never made it there, but it was still magical to sit in such a historical place.

Napoleon was famous, not only for his political career, but for his love life as well. His relationship with Josephine (whose first name was actually Rose, but Napoleon preferred her middle name) was tumultuous. Still Napoleon, like everything else he was able to conquer in life, conquered the way of the woo. He wrote Josephine love letters that, to this day, are known as some of the most beautiful and eloquent of all time.

Napoleon entered into courtship with Josephine knowing he wanted an older woman, a wealthy woman. She was "chosen" like so many wives were back in that time: not based on love, but practicality and advancement.

However, Napoleon quickly fell in love. Josephine did not. In fact, she detested him at the beginning. Napoleon was faithfully devoted; she was not. Napoleon wrote letter after letter, pouring out his heart and his desire for her. Building the woo, one brick at a time, that even a lifetime of betrayals and ups and downs could never fully destroy. It wasn't until after Napoleon was made aware of Josephine's indiscretions that his acts of wooing ceased.

* ● *

Ironically, it was then that Josephine began to love him, but it was a day late and a dollar short. Napoleon eventually divorced Josephine, but he never stopped taking care of her.

Now, you might be wondering why anyone would give all they can to a person, when chances are it would end up like Napoleon and Josephine? In my humble opinion, you don't get to claim love or that you have the slightest idea what it is, until you are faced with the choice of whether you can love someone despite an epic failure on their part. You realize this once you have experienced the agony of being hurt so deeply after you have invested so much, and still the love goes deeper than the hurt. Also, even though your relationship might change by ending, you choose to find the good in what you once saw as only good; this is when you can wave the "I know what love is" flag. When you choose to let the love change into a new way of relating to each other, just as Napoleon and Josephine did. It is about making the effort and seeing it through to the end, no matter how many changes--beginnings and ending—accompany that commitment.

Saying that you know what love is before you have ever been truly vulnerable is like making YouTube videos and calling yourself a director. Or self-paid photo sessions after which you call yourself a model? Or...and I am speaking to myself here, writing a blog and calling yourself an author. It is so easy to claim

* ● *

a title. But when it comes down to it, love demands more than that. Human connection does too. It takes more than the facade of "connection." That is what we are talking about here. Separating the faux connection from the real connection.

Wooing takes more than a ten second text message. It takes more than clicking 'like' on a person's post. It takes more than tweets. It takes more than cocktails and a good time. It takes more than the internet. It takes more than a public proclamation of going from "single", to "it's complicated", to "in a relationship with..."

So what is wooing? The old school woo. An example might be this:

Step number one: find someone woo worthy (we will discuss this further in the next chapter).

Step number two: commit. Commit to the gestation of this one little connection. Commit to focusing your attention on it singularly. Commit to listening, learning and then taking appropriate steps in pursuing that connection based on what you know and learn from this person. Commit to yourself that you will give it a fighting chance. You will try. You will put forth effort. You will sacrifice the time necessary. You will make room in your day, your thoughts and your plans, to actively woo this person. Let go of all the loose ends you have hanging with all these little, mini banter sessions you have with the ten different people you are texting on a given day. Commit to one. One.

Step number three: decide now that whatever you do, you will not count the cost. Because when you are a wooer, there are no costs. You are a millionaire of woo. You have plenty of woo to spend. You enjoy the process. The imagination it takes and the effort it takes. You have fun in seeing your effort make that person smile, happy, open....yours.

If you have to drive an hour just to see a person that you committed to seeing, even if you have to wake up at the crack of dawn, do it. Stand by your word. Or better yet, remember what it feels like to actually want to go the extra mile. Just because you may have no desire to go the extra mile for someone you meet doesn't mean that person isn't worth it. You could go around forever saying you just haven't found the one that makes you want to, when truth is, you are probably so desensitized that you have so little feeling left that you can't even know if you have found that one. That is what not allowing emotional connections does to a person. It either makes you completely lethargic or makes you have ADD when it comes to being able to focus on someone and commit to wooing them. Either way, you don't have the desire or the focus.

If you look back at how much the world has changed since you were in high school...how much it has changed since your parent's generation, you will begin to understand the reasons we are all floundering in our relationships. We've gotten caught up in a current that is not only moving swiftly, but is shallow as well. Its force is so strong that it is not possible to keep your footing. Technology is that current. If woo were a superpower, then technology would be the kryptonite.

And here is why:

Bottom line, you cannot replace a flesh and blood, one- on-one connection with a technological one. You can't replace the feeling you get when you hear someone's voice at the other end of the line, their tone, their inflection. You can't replace the feeling of having that person sit less than two feet in front of you with a Skype call or FaceTime.

We are substituting true connection with a shallow, disconnected version of it. Our minds may be fooled; obviously they are fooled, but you can't fool your heart. That is the very thing we are trying to destroy, extract, cut out as if it were a cancer. The heart, the healthy emotion of things, the frightening outcome ahead if we don't recognize and stop this now is that without heart and emotion... we can no longer create something beautiful in this world. Look at babies. They technically have everything they need to survive: breath, food, shelter, yet sometimes, they still don't thrive. This is known as "failure to thrive." Similarly, if we remove the heart from things, we will see all the beauty in our world die. The arts, creativity, music, romance, color, gratitude, peace, selflessness...

It may sound like doomsday, but it is also the truth. The good news is, it's also easy to fix. The technological current may be strong, but the true connection current is stronger. Instead of living like little self-absorbed, reality TV stars, we must go back to the basics and remember what really counts.

This was my epiphany strolling through the French Quarter. It took a city that was torn apart and put back together again, better than it was before, to make me realize that humans are at the same crossroads. We can watch as it all gets destroyed, then walk away and abandon it. Or, we can wait for someone else to come along, the FEMA of human connections, and we all know what happens with that. If we wait on someone else to fix our problems, we are going to be sitting in the middle of the debris of our lives for a very long time. Or, we can use what it takes to rebuild it, ourselves. That means taking what we knew of the old and bringing it into the 21st century. Not a replica, but building something with both the old and the new; something that can withstand the changes of our time, something that is even better than what we once knew.

Wooing is a good place to start rebuilding what has been demolished when it comes to communication and commitment. You may be confused about what constitutes woo. I know I was. I had gotten so used to being in control, the one who made the effort. I didn't have the time or patience

* ● *

to sit around and wait for someone else to do it. The guys I met were either too intimidated or lazy to take any initiative in the relationship, until I finally stopped expecting it. These guys fell into two extremes: the ones who made no effort and the ones who went overboard in the name of "love" (of course there were always strings attached).

None of these scenes fall under the category of woo.

Examples of my faux woo suitors:

1. Guys that claim they are in love with me and would do anything for me. As soon as I tell them I don't feel the same, but honor their feelings and friendship, they disappear. Where did all that love go? Hmm...

2. I had one man offer to invest in my business. He sought me out in the name of 'I believe in your talent and your business and want to be a partner.' I knew something was fishy, so repeatedly said no to his offers of a "partnership." Eventually he got so frustrated he blurted out, "What's a guy got to do to see you naked??!" Yep. We went from I want to invest as a business partner to naked in a just a few "No, thank you's". This is not business woo (woo is not only for romantic scenarios).

3. How about that guy that always wants to meet for coffee or a drink, claims he is really into you, so you meet for coffee only to endure an hour of him talking nonstop about himself as he blows cigarette smoke in your face. Then can't understand why you just see him as a friend. But, he thinks because he offered to pay for the drink...

4. Guys that text message to say they can't make it. Guys that would only surprise you with effort if it were your birthday or Christmas. Guys that have never once picked up the phone to call you, yet want you to say yes to a date.

These are just some examples. Now for you guys...the girl faux wooers:

1. The girl that allows you to buy her drinks and dinner with no intention whatsoever of dating you. However, she never shares that fact with you.

2. The girl who met you yesterday, meets you tonight for drinks and is leaving your bed tomorrow morning for work. It happens, yes, and I am not saying that is wrong. However, if she is so emotionally disconnected that she just handled you like you have handled women in the past? There's your sign.

3. The girl that seems to be paying attention but is really just thinking of what she is going to say to interrupt you.

4. The girl who works harder on her spray tan than she does on cultivating her inner qualities.

5. The girl that you have to wear that mask with...you know the one...the one that every man wears around his girl and takes off when he is around his guy friends. If you can't be real, how will that relationship ever be more than the half-truths it is built on? How exhausting it must be...

Here are words that are in conjunction with the word woo: effort, commitment, patience, assertion, listening, understanding, giving, sacrifice, desire, action, attention, focus, passion, creativity, romance, gestures, honesty, bravery, bravado, loyalty.

Acts of woo include: phone calls, visits, handwritten letters, gifts (grand or small), poems, music, sharing likes, being emotionally available, listening, respect, making dinner instead of going out, learning how to make your man's favorite drink, learning what your girl's favorite color is and surprising her with anything in that color...just showing her you heard her and you cared enough. It's that simple. It goes on and on.

Men, do you really want to know what women want? Look at the mind-blowing success of the Twilight books and movies. People want to make fun, but a large part of the population jumped on board that crazy train. I have walked into militantly feminist homes and seen one of the books tucked into a corner. Most women have read it, and the ones who make fun of it publicly are sneaking into the matinee while everyone else is at work.

So what is it about this story that drives women wild? I can tell you this much: it isn't Robert Pattinson. It is LOYALTY, plain and simple. "Edward" is what every woman wants, period. A man so loyal, so captivated, so into one woman. He is her protector. He is her friend. He is passionately into her. He adores her. He sacrifices for her. He denies himself for her. No other woman matters, or can even make him look her way. This, men, is what every single woman longs for but rarely gets, especially these days, Unrealistic? Yes. This is not how men are made. But I do believe every man has all of these characteristics in them. Most just feed the other characteristics more, so these get put on the back burner or burn out altogether. Men have become lazy. It is the truth. And women have been a big reason why. But we'll get into that later.

Now, women, what is it you think men want? Well, just as you think it would be heaven for a man to love you the way Edward loves Bella, most men think it would be heaven to be seen as good as

Edward in Twilight. To know they aren't disappointing you, or even have the potential to disappoint you. To be accepted for who they are, and not in a "you poor thing" kind of way, but in a "you are perfect to me just the way you are" way. We women think we know best: tough love, nagging, say it enough times and he will break. No. He will only distance himself from true intimacy while pretending to be something he is not.

That said, wooing is simply the act of laying down what you think you know about the opposite sex, then being willing to truly listen, learn, accept and court that person passionately.

The art of woo. Are you ready to become an artist?

two
Woo
Worthy

"You know what luck is? Luck is believing you're lucky, that's all. To hold a front position in this rat-race, you've got to believe you are lucky."

— A Streetcar Named Desire

Lucky. I've heard it used in so many different ways, from "I hope I get lucky tonight" to "I am so very lucky to have him."

Driving down St. Charles Avenue on a sunny October day, it was me saying, "Man, these people are lucky." And I was thinking that in more ways than one. From, "Man, these people are lucky their gigantic mansions didn't get flooded," to "Man, these people are lucky to have survived the recession." And then there was, "Man, I am lucky I don't have to take care of these lawns."

But in this chapter, "lucky", for the dames, means: "Luck be a lady tonight." And for the gents: "Luck is what happens when preparation meets opportunity." One's a song written by Frank Loesser and the other, a quote by Seneca (a Roman philosopher).

Being woo worthy is just as important for the women as it is for the men. It is cleaning yourself up a bit. Making sure all your life ducks are in a row. Having the rectitude to represent the real you in the best way you can. It is what sets you apart from the rest of the pack. It doesn't mean portraying yourself as perfect, or even feeling that you have to be perfect. It is more about common sense. The common sense to know who you are and live it.

I know men that have been way less than woo worthy. I know men that have slept around, used girls and treated women like dirt. It's not until they find one girl that they fall for that they finally clean their acts up in attempts to become woo worthy. A lot of times it works, because for every bad boy out there, there is a good woman waiting to squire them into the realm of woo worthiness. With that said, even a man who has ex- lovers living on every other street in his city has the opportunity to become woo worthy.

Unfortunately, women aren't so lucky. Even in this day and age we are judged much more harshly. Most of the time we have to clean up our acts before meeting that one. It is not fair, but it is where human-created stigmas and generations of beliefs still play out on the battlefield of the sexes. In the day and age we are living in, social stigmas concerning a woman's sexuality have lessened greatly compared to other generations and depending on many factors, but we still have a long way to go.

We are still living with double standards, and both sexes still hold on to them, come hell or high water. They are ingrained in us and passed down from generation to generation. Let's take two of the main double standards and see if there is anything useful we can extract from them.

One of the main double standards that men hold is the "what's good for the goose is not good for the gander" mentality. They convince themselves that "men will be men", and that's an unspoken truth they hold amongst each other. If a woman does as they do, she is labeled "not marriage material." Men are willing to sleep with any kind of woman, but only willing to marry one kind. What they consider to be the "good" kind. Some men would argue with this, but it is a general truth that most men could never handle what they dish out on a daily basis.

The origins of why they most men can't take what they dish out go back as far as the imbalance of equality through the centuries. A woman's whole life, provision, and security depended on a man. Therefore, men obviously held the upper hand for centuries where their behavior was concerned.

On the other hand, women also have double standards, one being that they expect men to know and understand everything about them. They expect men to read their minds, find the hidden meaning behind their words, and live in a constant awareness of their emotional needs. However, most women are not willing to do the same for men. They turn a blind eye and an upturned nose to the truth of who the man really is: his thinking, his needs, and his biology. Even if they do see the truth, they often ignore this and project their ideals onto him. The man, of course, usually falls short of this and then nagging ensues, followed by an eventual surrender to the ideal on the man's part. This leads to the man playing out a role every day which is only truly stripped away and made bare when he is out with a group of guys. That is why so many guys crave and love their "guy time." It is a chance to drop the facade they wear on a daily basis in their relationship, which they do in in an attempt to not rock the boat.

Anything to avoid confrontation and the accountability of looking at themselves and bettering themselves on more emotional levels.

These double standards often do more harm than good, but what if we could find something positive as well? Something we can take from them so that the centuries of their existence can have a little good karma mixed in with the bad? Like a karmic swirl. Let's do a little PR spin on double standards, shall we?

What is woo worthiness: women maintaining their 21st century freedoms of sexuality and expression, while still retaining their self-respect. Women making the decision that they are going to take off their "how I want to see men" glasses and put on their "I want to see the real man and not impale him for it" glasses. Women being real. Women making the decision to realize that men are hunters. If this is the case, as proven through centuries of behavior, why then would women make it so very easy for a man to get to know them? Experience them? Be intimate with them? When you respect yourself you know your worth.

For men, woo worthiness means letting go of their hypocritical tendencies and accepting that there is more to a woman than her sexuality. He stops seeing women as interchangeable and expendable. He lays down his male ego long enough to truly get to know a woman for all that she is and he pursues and treats her the way a lady deserves to be treated. With that, he allows himself to drop the mimic of the mindset of a woman simply to have peace in the relationship and truly allows himself to admit the truth of his needs and who he is. By doing this, he would find that he actually does get in touch with the deeper emotional parts of himself...simply because they are not covered up in layers of BS. It is like the quote from the great Anais Nin: "When others asked the truth of me, I was convinced it was not the truth they wanted, but an illusion that they could bear to live with." The day we all decide to live the truth of who we are is the day the illusions dissipate and we become woo worthy.

Now we get to what woo worthiness is not. Camera phones, for example. Great invention. Not so great for woo worthiness. Like most women, I fell for it at first. Getting ready on a Friday night with the theme song, "Man, I feel like a woman," blaring in my head. I looked at myself in the mirror, would take my phone and click, capture that pose. Post that up on Facebook. Everyone has done it. Or you send a flirty picture off to that guy you are seeing or are interested in. Harmless, right? Maybe, maybe not.

For guys, the scenario is a little bit different. You're out on a Saturday night with your boys. You have so much alcohol in you that the only difference between you and a keg is the spigot. You take that shot with those girls standing next to you, the ones with so many beads around their necks that they're about to fall over.

Yeah...this is not woo worthy.

On the day I woke up and looked at my own woo worthiness, I deleted almost every, "Hey, don't I look cute?," "Hey, check out my new dress," "Man, I feel like a woman" shot I had ever taken. I meant no harm with them, but they in no way reflected my basic morals or choices in life. They were open doors to misconceptions and judgments that cause misunderstandings. Remember what I said in the first chapter? We live in a time when people form an impression within the first three seconds of meeting you. The moment they get home, or maybe even in the bathroom at the restaurant or gym or wherever, they are already Googling your name, pulling up every bit of innocent fun you have ever posted for the world to see.

It isn't about censoring yourself or your fun, it is about being selective on what you choose to share on a public level to the people in your life that aren't necessarily part of your life at all. A little privacy is sexy. Remember that.

If that guy you are interested in still holds on to that double standard I spoke of earlier, even in the slightest most unconscious way, his first ignorant thought is going to be that you send these pictures to every guy. Even though you have had a total of two boyfriends in five years time and are just letting loose for once in your life. He isn't going to see that. He's going to think on autopilot, which is "if she sent this to me, she must do this all the time." Never once thinking of the countless times he may have pulled a Brett Favre on numerous, tipsy occasions. In fact, that is what human nature does to a person who is not 100% truthful and accepting of who they are as people; what you do, you will project onto others. If you have not accepted and been openly truthful about who you are as a person, then you will not expect it from others Look at that person in your life, and we have all seen this kind at one point or another, that is so insanely jealous and come to find out, that very person is the one living that "double life" of cheating or messing around all the while claiming they aren't capable of it. That is just one example. Projection...when you begin to recognize when you do it to a person, you begin to see yourself for what you have tried to deny and ignore is there. This is part of woo worthiness.

Women also judge books by their covers. Which came first, the chicken or the camera? It is cowardly to judge a person before really knowing them. But it is also a person's responsibility to be aware of how they are presenting themselves. You don't have to live for other people's approval, obviously. But you do have to hold some self-respect.

When I first started writing I created a blog. My mentor told me that I needed to come up with a very clever name, something intriguing and catchy enough that it would drive traffic to the site. One night, while writing in bed (which is where I usually find myself writing), I came up with a name that had the word "bedroom" in it. To me, my bedroom is where I lay my soul out. Where I sit with no make-up on, in my pajamas, typing away as I pour out my soul's contents. I also knew that people would read that name and think it was something completely different and that would make them click on it too.

What an ignorant thought! Never in my life had people had such misconceptions of me. I had men not ask me out because they saw the name and misunderstood it. I had women say, "Oh my, are you a sex writer?" WHAT??? I would get so frustrated that none of these people even took the time to click on the link, read my writing and see that it was simply about life-- all of it. So you have to think of these things and their consequences before you throw something out for all the world to see and make a judgment of. Sure, you really shouldn't care what people think. This is true. However, we live in a world of judgment. It is the truth. We size people up every second of every day, even if not consciously doing so. Our relationships, communication, trust and therefore, openness are based on these judgments.

It really is no different than less modern times when in courting a person, you depended on what was known of the reputation of the family and of that person. In a now modern age, we find out about a person through the internet. Reputation, whether established or not, is judged from what is found on that person. How that person acts and communicates in social media. In a lot of ways it is unfair, but it is true of how we are sized up these days. That is why it comes down to a "worth issue." If you have higher self-esteem and know you are worth something, you present yourself in a respectful manner. It just is the case. Not a sloppy manner. Not a questionable manner. You show respect in yourself and your reputation first and foremost. This doesn't mean living for the approval of other people. It just means having some dignity or selectiveness in what you make public.

It comes down to the fact that if you have something of worth, you take care of it. You present it in a way that shows you value it. You protect it.

Think of St. Charles Avenue. If you have never been to New Orleans, just Google it. Immaculate yards, stunning wraparound porches, elegant wrought iron fences. These houses are owned by the wealthy. They are well taken care of. They represent the grander things in life. They make a statement. That statement being, "I am worth something." None of them are doing open tours to the public of "Hey, come in and see every little thing we love and have collected over the years including our decor and what we wear to bed at night."

Privacy is a component of woo worthiness. With privacy comes a shroud of mystery, and mystery woos woo, if that makes sense. Mystery is the "come hither" beckoning to the wooer, the lure. And it isn't about hiding something. It is about having a little subtlety. I can say this because I learned lessons in my days of being on the front lines of the online community. Those who have become friends with me through social media, whether by following my writing or through mutual Facebook friends, have all said they were surprised to discover certain parts of my personality that the public is not privy to. That's the way it should be. Facebook, Twitter, and all the other forums should not be the main extension of your personality. They should be the CliffsNotes, not the full story. And a person who is only willing to take the time for the CliffsNotes version and then make judgments from that, is not a Woo Worthy person.

When you are woo worthy, you are wealthy, just like the owners of those houses on St. Charles Avenue. When you are woo worthy, you protect that wealth with privacy. No one protects their privacy more than the rich. It is true. How rich are you on the inside? What's your woo worth? Do you spend time and resources to make sure you are just as presentable and clean on the inside as the outside? In this information age, can you balance yourself between the old school way of living and the technological ways of today and still be private but open?

Luck be a lady tonight. I think some women have forgotten what it means to be a lady. Or maybe it is because there is no point of reference anymore. We have evolved too far beyond the old definition of a "lady", which was essentially another word for repressed. The challenge has become, how do we define a lady today?

So, what is a lady? Is it the version of a woman who doesn't speak until spoken to? Is it a version of a tightly wound woman in her kitchen with red lipstick and the cutest dress you have ever seen? Is it a version of a woman in the 1920's glitter and glam? Is it a woman in a muddy field, dancing barefoot while giving love freely? Is it a woman being pulled around by her hair off in some cave? Or is it the woman of today that has more lovers than years of life behind her and has given up the expectation or even desire to be courted or have a mutually respectful relationship?

Being a lady in the 21st century comes down to maintaining control where control is no longer expected. It is about exposing some parts of yourself to the outside world, while keeping other parts private. It is about being yourself, but not overdoing it. It is about balance. That is a lady these days: taking all the definitions of womanhood down the centuries, and keeping the good from each one, all the while respecting the freedom we have now, thanks to the generations of women before us who fought for it.

So take that picture of yourself in that cute little dress next weekend, but don't do it every other day. Post on Facebook and tweet away, but also read a book and send handwritten letters too. Work on the deep things as well as the surface things. Balance it. Clean it up a bit. If there are things floating around out there that look like pictures from a trip to Vegas-- when you weren't even in Vegas--clean it up.

Are you a technology junkie, or teetering on the edge? Do you spend more time texting than seeing the things around you? Do you find it hard to drive without texting? Do you have to look at your phone every few seconds to see if you have anything new?

If you can't sit across from someone in a restaurant without having your phone out, this is a clear sign that you need balance in your life. You need to start paying attention to your inside more than your technology. I have to keep myself in check with this all the time.

Balance is also import for women of older generations who now find themselves single. If you have no idea how to use Facebook or read a text, much less send one, you will have to learn. Balance it. Expand your horizons. Learn how to text so when that man sends you one, you can respond. It goes both ways, and the only factor that creates woo worthiness is the balance between the two.

Taking the time to connect with yourself, first and foremost, sets you on a woo worthy path. When someone is in touch with the core part of themselves it is apparent the moment they walk into a room. They stand out among the shallow people of the world. You know those people who remind you of a sand bar--close to shore: water covers it, but when you get there you see there is no depth. This is how a lot of people are these days, and it's because no one works on the inside anymore.

Video games and TV and phones and chatting and texting, all these things distract us from ever focusing on anything other than the superficial. They are attention-grabbing thieves of time that make something as beautiful as a sunset appear as dull as a PBS pledge drive, simply because it's not in HD with the ability to text you as it's going down. It certainly takes away any moments of self-reflection that might help us know ourselves better. And it is unrealistic to think someone— whether a woman or a man--who doesn't even know themselves is going to take the time to really get to know you. Again, it comes down to what you place value on. If you don't really care about inner growth, then the woo isn't for you.

Now, let's get to luck. Luck, no matter which way you spin it, is about being in the right place at the right time. For some, that is determination. For others, it is intuition. And for most, it means fate, something you have no control over. Everyone wants to be lucky in love. But no one wants to have to make the effort to ensure that. They want it to magically fall from the sky. Like a lightning bolt or lucky lotto numbers.

Luck is what happens when preparation meets opportunity. This is where so many men eliminate themselves from the lineup. Opportunity comes and they are like deer in the headlights. Why? Because they have not prepared. No inner work. No self-growth. They have done absolutely nothing to expand their opinions or even their understanding of how women think and what they want. Or to be emotionally available because they are open and honest with themselves and the ones around them.

Men have been putting their heads in the sand when it comes to the changes that the 21st century has brought to the playing field. That is to say: a more even playing field. Most don't want to have to evolve beyond the times when women needed them for basic survival and a roof over their head. Lord, men got away with murder back then! They could do whatever they wanted, whenever they wanted. They didn't have to be anything other than providers. This is what they considered to be a "good" partner. This is why women were put in such a position in the first place: it was easier on the fragile male ego. I am not hating on men here. I am stating simple fact. Men used to get away with not working on themselves, but not anymore.

The men who are still doing this today are men who are feeding the perpetual "all I do is hook-up" cycle. They really can't get a woo worthy woman without that inner preparation we are speaking of. And even if they do, it is only until the moment that woo worthy woman wakes up to see the inner pauper of a man she has been dressing up as a king. Most woo worthy women have their sights aimed higher. So the men settle for the less than woo-worthy-women. And what we have as a result is a society embracing sex as a sport and not something of value.

Women who have traded in their self-respect and self- esteem for the "I am no longer going to be vulnerable to men" option are hooking up like rabbits as well. They are no better than the men who have traded the satisfaction that comes with self-improvement and true commitment for the "I am going to use up as many of these opportunities as I can and stay right where I am at. Whowants all the work commitment takes anyway?" option.

So now you have men that hook up all the time. You have women that hook up all the time. You have people in double digits and triple digits when it comes to sexual partners. And sex is no longer something that is considered sacred. Sacred in the sense that you don't just hand it out like sticks of gum to people who ask for it. In my circle of my friends, I have the lowest number of partners, including those friends who are ten years younger than me. How can this be? I have guy friends that ten years ago could never get laid and now they are like their own little rock stars. Just because women have changed the game and become less scrupulous. But even after all that, it is still women who I hear cry and get hurt, even when they went into it knowing exactly what they were doing. Men and women both contribute to this erosion of respect, and with each hook up they chip away a little bit more at their ability to truly connect and be intimate with a person.

One way men can become woo worthy is to let go of the archaic ways of thinking. If you are going to do things- such as apply the double standard to sexuality, don't expect something different from a woman. Take responsibility for your actions. If you wouldn't want it done to you - such as cheating, etc., then think a little next time before choosing something. A man who is confident in himself and has a balanced ego will not find a woman's sexuality a threat. He won't judge a woman for the same sexual behavior he engages in. He will be choosy, of course. But men who have been lapping up--for lack of a better word--the free love being thrown all around have no right to judge.

If you are a man who seeks to become woo worthy, you will learn to communicate a little deeper, instead of disappearing at the first sight of conflict. You will open up and be honest with yourself instead of just ignoring how you really think about something. This is all preparation, because it removes the fragile ego armor, one little kink at a time, until you are vulnerable enough to touch and feel. And this is what women truly want. A woo worthy woman wants to be real and wants her man to be real. That alone takes an experience to a deeper level and not just hook up. A woo worthy woman wants to get to know you, every part, and not judge. A true woo worthy woman will lay every weapon down before you even begin to remove that armor. She won't criticize or try to make you wrong for being different than her. She won't try to make you into a hairier version of herself.

That's right. This is how women woo men: acceptance. And we will get further into that in another chapter. But for now, these are the basics in becoming woo worthy. Here is the thing, if you

* ● *

wanted to be one of the lazy, me-me-me humans taking over this world today, you would not even be reading this book. So there is a part of you that wants to woo. You want a better result out of what you have been giving and getting in return. There is a part of you that recognizes there has to be a better way than what the world is going with. This alone qualifies you for woo worthiness.

To be woo worthy, both men and women, you have to be like those grand mansions on Saint Charles Avenue. You have to be old school, historical but newly renovated.

You can have the character of those original hardwood floors and doors. But you need new pipes and electrical wiring. You take the old and enhance it with the new. It is called restoration.

A house is worthy of restoration when it has quality craftsmanship that makes it stand out as unique. The architectural integrity is intact. Just like a person.

You are woo worthy when you combine the old and the new, when you are interesting and you have something worth preserving. Something unique and different from the rest standing around you. You are like one of those mansions on Saint Charles Avenue, with your architectural integrity blaring like a neon light saying, "I am money." You respect your "house" and with that respect, you guard it.

Are you money? Then start acting like it. That is all woo worthy is, acting your worth. And no one can determine your worth but you. Even if you grew up poor, you can have anything you believe you can have. Even if you have acted like a pimp or a prostitute in the past, you can still rediscover your true worth and become woo worthy. Anyone can.

It only takes a choice. Having enough self-respect that you take the reins and start creating what it is you truly want in life, instead of going with the mindless flow that everyone else is in. Choosing to be an individual. Choosing to be different from the status quo. Choose to make changes, restore the inside, start gutting it out, doing the hard work to make it a jewel that leaves an impression on this planet.

Being woo worthy is also about realizing you are worth wooing, that you do in fact want to be wooed. If you don't hold those standards or desires for yourself, no one else is going to. You can't just be satisfied with the superficial way of connecting today. You have to want more, and with that, you have to be willing to give more, too. Ladies, you can't accept that date invitation through a Facebook message and then wonder why the guy isn't stellar in the romance department. You can't exchange thousands of texts with a guy and then get disappointed when you realize you really don't know him at all. Guys, you can't expect a girl to meet you for drinks on the first date, A) without first calling (not texting) to ask her out, or B) asking her to meet you for cocktails at 9 pm, without having first asked her for a meal or something else that happens before 9 pm.

After all, guys, why would you want to pursue a girl that way? And girls, why would you want to be pursued that way? If it is because you're a guy who wants the easiest way to get the results you are looking for, then be honest about that. Girls, if it's because your self-esteem has been so badly trampled by the experiences with the men in your past that you no longer expect anything better for yourself, then be honest about that. Be honest and clean it up to woo worthiness. It's that simple.

Ultimately, it comes down to how much worth you place on yourself. Once you begin making choices from a place of high self-worth everything will begin to fall into place. You will make yourself presentable and respectful. You won't let that lawn be overgrown or the paint to fade.

You will fix something the moment it breaks, instead of letting it go. You will make sure your place is clean and your "house" is a reflection of your worth.

You will be wise about who you invite inside your "home." You will take the precautions necessary to protect and keep it safe. You will guard the things you find valuable. You will open your doors to those who you want to welcome. You will let those come and sit at your table. You will shelter someone in need. You will feed someone who is hungry. You will leave a light on so someone can find their way home. You will feel

* * *

worth something because you have chosen to be worth something.

Think of it like taking a streetcar down the Avenue, and your mouth gapes open as you point to the magnificence of the sites you are seeing; this is what being woo worthy is. You walk in that room and everyone knows it. They stop and notice, because you exude worth. You exude a genuine quality and confidence. You know yourself, have taken the time to work on what needs work, and are a landmark because of it.

You are now woo worthy.

Three
Beware of
WOOves in
Sheep's Clothing

Oh, the lure of the bad boy. And now, in the 21st century, the bad girl as well. There have always been bad girls, but in today's society they are no longer enjoyed behind closed doors. Today, you have that one that everyone but you can see is trouble and yet you openly invest in this person not just for pleasure, but to actually try and hook. Oh the insanity of it all. Even so, a bad boy and a bad girl are hard to resist when you are making relationship decisions from what I call "needyville central." That place inside yourself that overrides logical thinking in order to feed a pattern. How many people on this planet "need" people to treat them badly? A lot more than you think. The ones that have loved themselves enough to turn that need into actual desire for someone to treat them with respect are few and far between. Just look at what most are willing to put up with on an everyday basis. The drama and the give and take played out every day like a little mini-series. It is an odd phenomenon when you try to actually suggest to those people how to stop the dramatic roller coaster they are on as they get defensive with you. That's when you know there is just no letting go of the bad boy/girl until you are ready to love yourself a little more. When you are in that stage in life, it is hard to resist the temptation to get on that roller coaster and enjoy the ride. Even if you feel like you are about to lose your lunch throughout it.

It is exceptionally difficult for women to resist a bad boy. One of the greatest traits of a woman is the capability to see the best in a man, even when the best in that man is playing hide and seek. The old saying, "Behind every great man, there's a great woman" testifies to this.

Sometimes, when a woman is capable of seeing the good when good is nowhere to be seen, it gives a man the courage to be his best. It's rare, of course, but it does sometimes turn out that way. Most of the time, however, this is not the case. It is almost like training puppies. I am not comparing men to dogs, I am just making an analogy here about the act of training. A woman will take a bad boy and train him enough not to "mess" in her house but that puppy will keep having accidents. All the while the woman continues to invest and show him the error of his ways. Usually after she has given blood, sweat, and tears to help him get it straight, he dumps her and ends up finding a woo worthy woman with whom he uses all his wonderful skills taught to him by the woman that took the time to invest in him, only to be left standing with nothing at the end. Long story short, women who choose these kinds of guys are like the perpetual foster puppy parent. They do all the hard work and the one that ends up getting him is the one that benefits.

I always hear the good men complaining about how they always get the short end, while women go for the bad boys. It frustrates them and I can totally understand why. In these moments I try to explain what it is that makes perfectly good women lose their perfectly good minds over men who are not perfectly good. Different women are attracted to many different things; however, there's one characteristic that is pretty much universally attractive. That universal trait is confidence. Whether a man is being good or bad, if he is acting with confidence, women like it. Of course, when it comes to true bad boys, that confidence goes hand in hand with more unsavory characteristics like mystery, seduction, charm, and unavailability.

* ● *

The biggest mistake men make when it comes to women is convincing themselves that women don't like a little challenge and mystery. Contrary to popular belief, women have and always will be hunters. On an everyday basis they are strategically protecting and providing for their own, manipulating circumstances to go in their direction. Women are masters of the hunt. So much so, they have convinced men for centuries of the opposite.

And so, men make the mistake of being predictable, of never trying to out-think the fox that is their partner. They just don't try. And women get bored. Then the cycle begins of either nagging to the point of certain death, or worst case scenario, a bad boy catches the eye of the woman starving for some challenge. Sometimes women want someone to take them and make them forget all the pressure and rules society has put on them (since conception) to be the "good girl." Sometimes they don't want to be the good girl...cue the bad boy's foot in the door.

Jean Laffite was a famous 19th century pirate and to make a long story short, he stole things and hurt people. Laffite considered himself to be a privateer and was genuinely hurt at being so "misunderstood." Does that change the fact that he was a thief and a killer? No, but during the War of 1812, when more men were needed in the Battle of New Orleans, Jean Laffite stepped up to the plate and became a hero of sorts. Even after imprisonment, he still fought. He never attacked an American ship. You might wonder how someone with such sketchy values was capable of also having such admirable ones? As crazy as it sounds, it is not as uncommon as you might think. Like Laffitte, many bad boys have passion, heart, and certain deeply held convictions, but they still wouldn't get the Man of the Year Award.

That is the downfall of women with the bad boy syndrome: the uncanny ability to see the good in men while ignoring their negative qualities. Using this "sixth sense" they create a faulty image better than Bruce Willis could; they begin to believe in that ghostly apparition, not the flesh and blood actions of the man. Sprinkle on a little of the Cinderella story they heard every day of their childhood, and you have the perfect recipe for heartbreak.

Fast forward to 2012: dating sites, social media, meet-up groups, pick-up artist schools and books. As if it were not difficult before to spot a bad boy, now women have to be savvier than an FBI profiler. Men, it is the same for you. The resources we have today that I spoke of in the first chapter, the ones that allow us to size up a person before we go and meet them for that first cup of coffee, are the same tools that are used to present a façade rather than a foundation.

I had a friend that met a man on a very popular and reputable dating site. On his profile and through correspondence, he stated that he did not drink and if he did, he had one or two beers at the most. So they would go out on dates and sure enough, he never had more than one or two beers. It wasn't until a year into their relationship that she found out he was a raging alcoholic. He would have six or seven beers before coming to get her for their dates. How did she find out? He asked her to watch his cat when he went away on a trip. She had to throw something in the trash cans outside. She lifted up the top of the trashcan to find it full of beer bottles and cans. His refrigerator was full of beer. In the freezer, the vodka fought with the Lean Cuisine for territory. He finally 'fessed up, but not until they had been together for two years.

So, how do we spot a bad boy or a bad girl when, in this day and age, we often meet someone's persona before we physically meet them? Well, I'm glad you asked! The answer: going back to the old school way of wooing. It's that easy. Not to say that people didn't get tricked, fooled, betrayed back then. Of course they did. But those time periods were more Pollyanna than today. People were not as skeptical. Again, the key to wooing today is to bring the old together with the new.

Bringing back old school wooing means: calling that person instead of always texting. Writing handwritten letters to each other. Going for walks in nature or doing something that doesn't have distractions, finding out what that person really enjoys and pursuing them based on that. Open up that car door for her. Walk her to her door. If you drive separately, make sure she got home okay. Truly listen to what she is saying and care enough to add to it. Girls, do something he would like to do for a change. Learn about sports. Allow comfortable moments of silence. Buy some lingerie. Do your hair instead of wearing it in its typical ponytail. Tell him how great he is, even though you have ten things you are aggravated with him about. Cook him a home-cooked meal for once instead of expecting to go out.

Now bring the new in. Balance being too trusting with being untrusting. Don't be gullible, but don't be too critical either. If you woo, you will find you get to really know a person. Not the image. Not the personality that comes out in text messages. Not the personality that shoots you an email or comments on your Facebook. If you go for a long walk, you connect better than if you are sitting in bar getting tipsy during happy hour. Cook at home once in a while and light some candles. Put on some music. Sit across from each other and really just enjoy each other's presence without cute waiters and hot hostesses and other people sitting around bringing distraction. It is time with just the two of you.

Do you know why pick-up artist schools, books, and websites have become so popular? Because there has been a breakdown in intimate connection, a weak link in the chain, and an opportunity to cash in on that breakdown. Female self worth is at an all time low. Men aren't any better off because they don't know how to really handle the changes. These changes have evened the playing field a bit in the sense that men no longer have absolute dominion over the women in their lives.

Women act like they don't expect anything from men anymore. They act like they are in control of their bodies and their sexuality. They act like they can be casual. Romance is not really a priority anymore. Meeting, hooking up, oops I did it again, on to the next one. This is the formula for today's connection. Yet, these same women go home and regret. They cry. They feel disappointed, like they are never going to find love. They go into a new connection acting like a ho, excuse the harshness, but then start saying "whoa" the moment a guy treats them as such. I am not talking about being a prude. I am talking about making the irresponsible choices that are based on low self-esteem; these are usually based on need and not want.

It is like handing someone a gun and saying, "Shoot me! Shoot me! Shoot me!" over and over. And when the person finally shoots you, you can't believe they just shot you! It is an insane cycle we are in right now and it has to be broken. The only way it can be done is by one person at a time coming to their senses about what they have been buying into, then choosing something different.

The divorce rate is the highest it has ever been. There are bread loaves with a longer shelf life than most relationships. I read recently that the average woman today has had more than 20 sexual partners. Of course, for men that number is higher. The magic number of dates before a new connection crashes and burns? Three. The statistics, if accurate, are really depressing.

So what do we do? Sit back and let it get worse? Go with the flow? Let go of any last residue of higher expectations or belief in love? Do we join 'em because we can't win? Do we just become more obsessed with the things that, if taken away, would send us into serious withdrawal? Think I'm kidding? Try leaving your phone at home while going to work. Try even leaving it in the car when you run into Starbucks for your Grande Mocha. Within two seconds you are going for it...where is it? In my purse...in my pocket.... Oh God, where is it?

Try getting in your car and not turning on music or talk radio. Silence. Your skin will start crawling after the first 60 seconds. Don't turn on your TV the moment you walk in the door. Sit in silence. Sit down on your couch, prop your feet up, try and read a book. You will be amazed at the flood of distractive thoughts that will overcome your mind the moment you try to do that. That is what has infiltrated our minds today. Enough distraction to make us emotionally disabled. Not to get into conspiracy theory with you, but it makes us like sheep. Distracted and fumbling all over each other. Not leaders. Not unique. Not self-aware. Disabled.

* ● *

Going back to wooing is not going to make it all perfect. But it does bring us back to our foundation. But even in wooing, you have to keep your eyes open for what I call the "WOOwolves."

What is a WOOwolf, you might be asking. A WOOwolf is a person that uses the disguise of wooing for superficial and deceptive motives. Like a wolf in sheep's clothing.

For example, the guy who seems to be such a gentlemen. He pursues and pursues and pursues. But it is all a game, to capture someone for egotistical purposes. It isn't rooted in integrity. It is to win, to conquer. Not out of respect, tenderness, or truly caring at all. The girl that seems interested and allows you to buy her dinner over and over again, stringing you along, acting like she thinks you hung the moon. The next day she's out with another guy who is buying her dinner and hanging the moon. She never once tells you she doesn't feel the same. She never once tells you she has zero interest in being with you.

This is all about waiting for the right time to pounce and get what they want. The moment they don't get what they want? They disappear. The moment they do get what they want? They disappear. Either way, they leave behind carnage.

How do you avoid all of this? It would be nice to have a chastity belt app for your phone that forbids you to text that specific WOOwolf back for a specific period. It would give you much-needed time to think, instead of giving in, only to regret it later. A chastity belt, under lock and key for at least 24 hours. So you can't text that guy or girl back after a couple margaritas, or after you haven't heard from them in a month and now suddenly they are in the game again. The key to the art of woo is knowing yourself enough to hear and sense your instincts about a person. Know what it is you truly want and need. Have enough self-esteem to stop trying to make something that isn't working work (I sucked at it). When you get to that place, no chastity belt app is needed!

But how do you start to get to know yourself? You have to stop the habitual thinking that has gotten you into this mess in the first place; the expectations based on how you are used to being treated, or what you are used to experiencing in relationships. One thing I do when someone doesn't treat me the way I want to be treated is say to myself: "Woo Dat!" It reminds me and makes me laugh. If I sense someone is not being 100% truthful or authentic with me, I say "Woo Dat!" If someone comes along and sends me a message on Facebook to ask me out for the first time, I say nope..."Woo Dat!"

Sounds silly, but it is a great reminder to become consciously aware when something is below the standards you have now (hopefully) set for yourself. It's kind of like having a rubber band around your wrist and snapping it every time you have a negative thought. It is just a reminder.

So what do you do if you had a date with someone and an hour before he is supposed to meet you, he texts and says he can't make it? Instead of sulking about a person who couldn't even pick up the phone to call, you say to yourself, "Woo Dat!!" and then you go do something nice for yourself. It is much easier said than done, but anything can eventually become habitual. It is our human nature to have habits. Why not develop positive ones?

Guys, if that this is the girl you have been pursuing and spending money on who plays dumb to your feelings and never once tells you she has any for you, yet takes all you have to offer her in the meantime. Or if she never takes the time to know what you really enjoy or would like to do and so you are always doing things her way in order to please her. I know it sounds stupid, guys, but just say, "Woo Dat!!" And say it with authority and enthusiasm, like you're the bomb. You are the best. You deserve the best. You are the best thing that person will ever come across.

The only way you are going to know the truth about whether a person is genuine or whether a person is a WOOwolf is if you have standards and that person meets them. If a person goes the extra mile, is emotionally available, shows respect, is willing to communicate deeper than a text message or an IM. If a person does their best not to disappoint you, and if they have to, they talk to you about it instead of being a coward and shrinking back into a shell of: "I can't answer your phone call, or text, or email because I can't handle it." If a person makes an effort to make you happy and do kind things for you, if they give you the honor of their time and really listen to you, it is then that you have yourself a genuine person.

It isn't as difficult as we make it. Attraction and hormones and the way we get all mixed up when we are into someone, this is what brings the haze and the fog so we can't quite see things for what they are. But if you have a solid foundation of strong self-esteem in place, then when these giddy, euphoric feelings take over, you'll have a compass to guide you, even when you can't see your hand in front of you.

No one is going to come along and do that for you or me. No other person is going to hold that magic key that suddenly makes everything right. No other person is going to come along and suddenly make it clear for you. They can help, for sure, but you and I are the only people that can do it for ourselves.

That is why wooing is such a healthy part of relationships. It takes integrity and caring about something, caring about you, and caring about someone else enough to make an effort; enough to be responsible for the outcome you want to have. Instead of placing it on another person, you bring it home to you. Wooing someone adds to the worth of that connection. Every time you woo, you add to it. You are building something here. Wooing is the foundation. Unless you have been hiding under a rock, most people have learned that if you have a bad foundation your whole building is susceptible to collapse; it certainly won't withstand a storm or years of weathering. If you start off with a strong foundation the rest of the building is stronger, more durable. It's the same in all relationships: romantic ones, friendships, business partnerships, and family.

When you woo then, even if the relationship ends, you have memories, like that person's handwriting in letters or notes. You have things to remember them by. You have something to hold. You have something tangible. Not just thousands of text messages full of superficial banter or a picture text to you from a night of being tipsy. Not just funny comments on funny posts. You'll have something of substance that doesn't just dissipate when the relationship is over.

WOOwolves aren't going to want to make the effort for a long period of time. Once they see that they aren't getting what they want they will get frustrated, make you out to be the bad guy and leave. But the one who is truly wooing you will woo for as long as it takes. So if you don't have the sixth sense to know a WOOwolf when you see one, you at least have the reassurance that one way or another they always show themselves in the end.

Eventually, you will be able to spot one from a mile away. Even if that person locks his or her sights on you, you will say to yourself, "Yep...you're a WOOwolf, so I'm NOT interested in going there with you." And it will be done. You won't have to waste life on the BS and the games that turn out the same way every time, unless you have become addicted to the game.

Did you know that scientists have linked rejection to the part of your brain that has addictive tendencies? Some Neurologists have gone as far as to say that romantic rejection has the same intensity in that part of the brain as cravings for cocaine. One study said that when participants were shown photographs of the partner that rejected them, it released the same "dopaminergic reward system evident in cocaine addiction." You can actually crave rejection, because it releases the same chemicals that addictive cravings and fulfilled cravings release.

If you have been on a perpetual path of bad boy/bad girl rejection-type connections, maybe you should take a look at that. It could be that you need to go to rejection rehab. You may need to really concentrate on choosing something different. As they say in The Twelve Steps, "acknowledging you have a problem is the first step." If you are a rejection junkie, just get a grip. Make different choices. Be vigilant when it comes to recognizing the WOOwolves.

Maybe Jean Laffite was to women in the 1800's what cocaine is to the drug scene today. Maybe that is what Denise Richards was attracted to in Charlie Sheen. Maybe being attracted to the bad boys and girls of today has the same effect. Who knows? I do know that in order to truly woo, you have to be true. Game playing and lack of authenticity don't blend with woo. Like oil and water, the two repel each other.

When you can recognize the WOOwolves in sheep's clothing that come tip-toeing into your life with roses and gestures, then you are a step closer to living life Woo Dat style. Guys, don't be so blinded by your intense desire to be with a girl that you overlook her motives. Girls, don't stick so many unreal post-it note projections on a guy that you cover up the real him in order to maintain the fantasy. Know what you want and how you want it. Give a person a chance to show themselves and when they truly do, believe them. Don't keep trying. Don't keep playing. Don't pretend. Be truthful and walk away. That frees you up for the person who is really willing to woo you right.

This is not easy. I will be the first to say it. I still fail at it, but I have come to accept that it comes down to a choice: I have to choose to let it go, to see it for what it is and have enough self-respect to do that. It is like anything else in life. You want a killer body, you take the time to work out. You want to be the best cello player there is, you take the time to practice every day. You want to make partner in your company, you work harder and more efficiently than anyone else there. You want to stop hurting and finally cut the string of bad connections trailing behind you? Make the choice, every day.

So, let me hear you say it...WOO DAT!!!

four
The Master Dater vs. The Master Baiter

"General, did you ever hear of Mosby?" "Yes, have you caught him?" "He has caught you."

- Captain John S. Mosby capturing General E.H. Stoughton-Civil War

The daters and the baiters. It really is simple, but attraction is the interference that scrambles the frequency. As a result, the normal, balanced, quasi-intelligent person will have a and lay down everything hoping that that person is really a dater. Why? When Shakespeare said, "love is blind" he really was onto something. Let's add living in the day and age of faux connections made via technology and we have lost the ability to call whether a person is a dater or a baiter even more than in Shakespeare's time. Back then love was just blind. Today, love is blind and too dumb. Dumb and dumber.

New Orleans's Audubon Park is not just a great place to walk or jog or lay on a blanket in the grass on a warm afternoon. It served as neutral ground for both the Confederate and the Union soldiers in the Civil War. Here is a little Civil War for Dummies: one of the causes of the Civil War was the fight between the slave states and the free states. The ones who fought for freedom realized that every person deserves respect. Every person deserves fair treatment. No one deserves to be owned by another. No one person is above another.

Audubon Park's grounds housed both the Confederate and the Union armies during the Civil War. Two opposing armies fighting with freedom hanging in the balance. If the world's relationships were compared to the neutral ground of Audubon Park--where two armies stand ready to battle each other--those armies would be baiters versus daters.

Just like in the Civil War, it comes down to a battle over control; whether for control of a city, a port, or a person. There were many things at stake in that war and the same is true for our analogy here. Where there stands a gross imbalance of things, where the end result will determine a person's freedom or slavery, this is where the battle is fought. In relationships there is most certainly a battle going on. You have those who believe in the equality and rights of every person and you have those who don't believe in anyone else's rights but their own.

* ● *

We discussed the Woowolves in the previous chapter. Those whose intentions are hidden beneath the box of candy or inside the bouquet of flowers or the heat of the pursuit they have been so adamantly committed to. It is at this point that you determine whether you have a baiter or a dater. The Woovolves are always baiters.

The baiters in the dating world today only do things designed to keep a person on the line. A baiter doesn't respect the other person equally. Rather, the baiter is only out to own. Their intentions are simple: keep that person on the hook until they get what they want out of them, then they dispose of them. A baiter does not believe in equality. A baiter does not have the ability to treat someone the way they would want to be treated.

A baiter is the guy or girl that seems hot and heavy at the beginning. You both text all day and into the night. You send a message, boom! They reply right back. You are thinking this person is so into you, you might even think this is going to grow into something. Then you stop hearing from them. The texts will dwindle down completely. You text now and it takes hours for a response, if at all. The baiter may even take a day to respond. Every few weeks though, you will probably get a check in. Which usually consists of something that could be mass sent, like a "What ya doing?" or "How ya been?" A baiter will comment every now and then on a post, right when you think you will never hear from them again. You will pick up the pace again in your faux communication, only to return to nothing.

A baiter will text and comment and reply back just enough to keep you there. Just in case he or she wants you down the line to fill some down-time when they have no one to give them what they need. A baiter will continue to reach out to you, but nothing like what they did at the beginning. Simply because they threw you back doesn't mean they don't want to catch you again. It is just but a sport to them. And you are nothing but that dumb fish that comes back and sees only the bait...not the hook that is about to tear into you again.

A baiter has no intention of dating you, of wooing you, of holding equal respect between the two of you. And here is the kicker: the times we get caught up with a baiter (and we all have at one point or another), we don't understand why that person has no respect for us. The sad truth is, we hold zero respect for ourselves if we allow their treatment. We cannot expect someone to respect us when we don't even respect ourselves enough to stop taking the bait.

The baiter sees it all as a game. They might not consciously be thinking to themselves it is a game, but they have placed you in a box of things to play with. Toys can be taken out, wound up to perform, and then thrown back in the box again when they lose interest.

* ● *

The bottom line is: if you don't have a dater, you have a baiter. There is no in between, unless you are choosing to be casual with your connections. If you do not want someone to date but rather have someone casually, then this does not apply to you. You are baiting yourself.

A dater is a person who, with everything they do, every communication they have with you, is showing their intent to actually build something with you. They won't be like little vampires feeding on you, only to split just when you think there might be some caring feelings growing. No, daters actually want to DATE you. They want to spend time with you.

At the end of a month with a dater, you will have memories of dinners and coffee dates and whatever else you did to get to know each other...you will have these memories to hold, not just a cell phone bill showing 1,000 text messages. You might have a handwritten note from your guy or gal. Or a card they dropped off at your door just to say "hey" or make you laugh. You won't just have a "lol" comment on a Facebook post or a tweet back.

There is nothing worse than the combination of a baiter and a dater getting together. Trust me, I know from experience. The baiter will have the notes and the letters and the little acts of wooing in their hands, which they will toss in the trash when it ends. The dater, on the other hand, will have a huge cell phone bill because and a blank profile pic next to

* ● *
67

all the comments made by the baiter because the dater has de-friended them or visa versa.

A dater will prove to you that they want you. They will not be a flash in the pan or a brilliant shooting star that leaves as fast as it came. No pun intended. A dater will do what it takes to pursue you with consistency and continue to do so after the connection grows. A dater will call you. A dater will ask how your day went. A dater will text you first, not just in reply. A dater will sit with you and not look at their phone every three seconds. A dater will be tangible, not invisible, not technical. A dater will be present. You can touch them, taste them, hear them, smell them, see them. They will not be just a bunch of words typed out.

A dater believes in equality. A dater holds respect for themselves and all people. And they won't pursue unless they truly want to know the person. That doesn't mean it always works out or that it doesn't end quickly. It just means they took the time to see if there was something there. There is a reciprocal feeling to it all, not an out- of-balance- feeding- frenzy- chase- and-devour feel to it.

A dater won't ask you out to "drinks" for the first date. A dater won't usually use the terms "hot" or "sexy" when telling you how you look on that first date. A dater will have spoken to you on the phone before that first date, not just by messaging. A dater will show you in every way possible that there is respect there, without even knowing you yet. That respect comes from the core value a dater holds, which is that all people deserve to be treated with respect. They also don't go around feeding on people like the baiters do. So, if they have even offered their time to get to know you, there is inherent respect there.

To a baiter, you hold no value. Your value is only as much as your ability to give them what they need at the time. Then you go back to being worthless to them. They will show you, with everything in them, that they consider you worthless. They won't reply back within an appropriate time frame. They will forget to answer you altogether, and when you ask them why they will say, "I forgot." Why did they forget? Because they couldn't care less. The text came through, they looked at it and didn't have an ounce of care in them to reply. So it isn't that they forgot, it is that nothing in them wanted to reply back to you. A baiter is only concerned with meeting their own need in the moment. If in that moment they don't want or need anything from you, you won't be hearing from them.

A baiter will text you to tell you they can't make it to your prearranged date. A baiter will not be willing to take you to dinner but will be willing to meet you for drinks after. A baiter will cuddle with you in the morning and let you make breakfast and give you a kiss as they walk out the door and you think, "Finally, this is going somewhere." Yeah, it's going somewhere all right. It's going to the next person he or she has on the line,

* ● *

because trust me: there is a whole string of them.

A dater will call you to tell you they are going to be late or need to change the date. A dater will meet you or pick you up for dinner. A dater will meet you in the afternoon for a walk, or coffee, or a volleyball game outside. A dater will go work out with you. A dater will cook with you. A dater will sit and listen as you share your favorite music with them. A dater will do whatever it takes to show you they are in it...even if that means listening to rap music when they love alternative.

A dater will tell the truth and communicate instead of disappearing. A dater will not have to comment on a post you wrote, because they actually talked to you in real life about that very thing. In fact, there probably won't be much social media interaction. Why would there be? You've got the real kind of interaction going on.

A dater does not see connecting as a battlefield like the baiter does. The baiter sees connecting as a chance to dominate and conquer. A chance to own a person whose only reason for being in their life is to serve them. A dater believes in equality. A baiter believes in inequality.

In your life you are like Audubon Park. Whom are you going to have on your grounds, setting up camp in your life, building their cooking fires and reloading their muskets: the daters or the baiters? This question goes for all types of relationships, not just romantic ones.

* ● *

These same principles apply in friendships and business partnerships, too. They also apply to people who are already in a relationship and want to make it last.

Let's touch on that sensitive subject for a bit. What about the people who are in committed relationships, but do just enough to keep that person from nagging them or leaving them? That is baiting. The people that no longer do what it takes to woo the other. They don't really care anymore to make an effort. They just do a little here and a little there... whatever keeps them from having to "hear it" at the end of the day.

How many people in committed relationships actually still actively pursue their other? Not many. Some people say, why should you have to? You are no longer chasing that person or trying to get into a relationship, you are in a relationship. Here is the common mistake people make when it comes to a committed relationship: just because you are with that person does not mean you have that person. You don't own anyone. Common sense dictates that if you want a person to stick around you won't just assume that you will have them around forever. Because our divorce rates show the opposite of that belief. If you want to keep it alive, whatever it may be for you, you have to actively woo for the duration of that relationship.

So now we know the difference between those

* * *

who are the masters of the date and the bait. But what about you, the master of your own life? You can know the difference all day long between the two, but if you don't have the self-worth to choose the dater, then this chapter has been worthless to you. At the end of the day, it doesn't come down to them, it comes down to you.

What are you willing to put up with and what do you think you deserve? Does receiving text messages instead of actual one-on-one time not really bother you? You will have as proportional an outcome as the standard you hold. If you have gotten so sucked in and so beaten down in the dating world of today, then I can pretty much bet most of your standards are as low as the last notch on the limbo pole you are willing to break your back to get under. Most of us have been there.

It really doesn't matter if you can distinguish between a dater and baiter if you can't even distinguish between what you really want and what you have been willing to accept. Again, Woo Dat! Every time you are in a place where you are excited that they texted you (even though you haven't heard from them in weeks and the last time you did they left you hanging after keeping you up until 2 am with the bing of the next message coming in) tell yourself "Woo Dat!" Next time he or she contacts you though you haven't laid eyes on them physically in forever, say "Woo Dat!" Say it over and over, until you start to really believe that you are worth wooing.

Don't fool yourself with banter. Convincing yourself that this flirtatious way of communicating once in a blue moon means that this person cares about you in the slightest won't do you any good. Don't eat crumbs off the floor and convince yourself you just had a five course meal. Don't bite when the bait gets tossed your way. You are the only one who can make the decision to pass it by.

Have you ever had someone who messages you, responds to you, flirts with you until you respond? The moment you let the wall down and act like you are into it too, they suddenly are as cool as ice? A common trait of a baiter. Yet, every time you reply back or bite, you are showing them that you are still falling for it. Hook, line, and sinker.

Don't be one of those people who has a baiter and yet tries to convince the world around you that you have a dater. Your friends see it. Everyone who cares about you can see it. Yet somehow you are convinced that because they do keep coming back, they must care for you. No. They only care for themselves, and they come back because you are their option at the time. Baiters are only as "wooful" as the choices presenting themselves in the moment. When they find themselves bored and in need of something, they think of you. You always bite. And yeah, they might be physically attracted to you or have a good time with you, but they don't want to do what it takes to date you. They just want to do what it takes to bait you.

Audubon Park is a beautiful landmark and reminder of the soldiers that once laid their heads down on that ground to sleep. They built their fires and had their pots and pans hanging over it to cook their meals. That land housed the wounded and the able. Soldiers who may or may not have lost their lives in battle set up camp at one time there. This beautiful park was a neutral ground for the weary to come back to after the fight and take refuge. Today, you get to decide who comes on your grounds and takes refuge. Who is allowed to stay a while...cook...sleep... recover and then go back into the battle ground called life. No one can occupy that space unless given permission by you. You are the sole owner of this space and are therefore solely responsible for who you allow to be there with you. In the world we live in, you have both the daters and the baiters wanting to set up camp on your grounds.

If you have any confusion at all as to what you want, or what you deserve. Or if you are not sure what you are worth, if you don't really believe there is an option because this is the way guys or girls are these days. If you used to wonder what is wrong with these people but now ask what is wrong with you. If you are a person that has a baiter and you have dressed them up as a dater. If you have convinced yourself that this person cares for you because they just don't let you go. If you are in a relationship and have a partner that does nothing to woo you or show you that they know you could choose to be with anyone, but choose them. If you are confused at all with whether or not the way a person is treating you is on par with your worth: I have two words for you. Woo Dat.

Woo Dat. Is texting you for booty call the same as wooing you? Nope. Woo Dat. Is someone disappearing for weeks at a time and the last time you heard from them you answered them back and then they didn't reply to you. Is that wooing? Nope. Woo Dat. Is someone who is willing to meet you at a bar but not have dinner with you wooing you? Nope. Woo Dat. Is a girl who will let you take her to dinner and pay for her, then give you the pat on the back at the end of the night for the 20th time considered wooing you? No guys, she is not. Woo Dat.

I think we have it down now. The Master Baiter and The Master Dater. Which one are you going to give your time to? Which one is going to get your attention, your affections, and your desire? Which one is going to get your romance and your loving? When it comes down to it, which one is going to get your heart? Because trust me, the baiters collect more hearts than the daters do.

So who will it be? The one who wants to be in your moments. Woo Dat. Now can you feel it?

* ● *

five
Counting
Coup

"Elevate those guns a little lower."

- Andrew Jackson

Oh, this is going to be a fun chapter. We're going to talk guns, war, Indians, vampires and hooking up. We are going to discuss strategy and honor. I am going to speak straight. So go ahead and open your mind a little and don't make me go Jack Nicholson on you. You CAN handle the truth.

Let's just go ahead and shoot straight now. In today's world sex has become a sport. It is a game. It is a show up, suit up (hopefully people are smart enough to do this) and win. Hit the showers and then go make a sandwich. That is as deep as it goes.

I know women who carry condoms in their purse "just in case." I know men who have a new partner at least once per week. I once was privy to a conversation with a 23 year old in which she told me she had she hooked up the night before with someone she had just met but could not remember if he had gone in through the back door...if you get my drift. I told you I was going to speak straight. I am in no way playing moral police here. One-night stands, meeting someone and going for it: this is no one's business but those choosing it, but can you remember a time where the one-night stand was actually considered a rarity? A time when you would reflect back on a night of passion with a stranger and live off of that stored memory like a camel in the desert storing water? For most, they were few and far between. Today, the one-night stand is common for the majority, while the intimate, relationship type of sex is a fading memory.

When a new stream of water is created it will carve out a new path for its force to flow through. Nothing can stop it and even stone will eventually wear out a groove for the water to pass through. A new stream of communication has been created on this planet, the technological one we have been discussing in the previous chapters. A new path has been forged. Sex is simply following that path and the result is intimacy that goes about as deep as a pothole. Just as a new path has been created, another path can be created. It just takes enough people wanting to. It is what is called the "mass consciousness." When enough minds are concentrating on the same thing, it will be. We are seeing a prime example of that happening now.

Anything as sacred (yes I am using so bold a word) as sex that can be described by the two words "hook-up," has lost its reverence. Even in the time of free love and the good ole' sexual revolution, there was still an attitude of respect in that free love. There was still an acknowledgment of "hey, I get that you have a soul and I have one too...so, peace man." Today it resembles carnage-- something you would see in a vampire novel or movie. You meet someone, you sink your teeth in, you get what you need, and you walk off to find your next victim.

The terms "sexy" and "hot" have replaced "beautiful" and "captivating." Let's not even get back into the infidelity statistics these days. It seems there is a large percentage of the population that could become professional hook-up star athletes.

Today, you walk into a bar—be it the nicest in town or the dive bar down the street—and if you are man there's a good chance you don't have to go home alone. Not these days. Women are on the prowl as much as men. On the other hand, most women don't even have to think about whether or not they might go home alone. Almost any woman could walk in anywhere and have anyone. Women could walk into Circle K and come out with a hook-up. All they have to do is state the desire. This isn't really something new. I guess the only new part in it is that there are a lot of women that are actually doing this. Okay, maybe not so much at Circle K, but you get what I am saying.

The state of sexuality today could be called "The Big Easy." Easy, easy, easy. And when it becomes that easy to give into your every whim, then how do you find the way to make it sacred again? How do men say "no" when they have a half a room of women willing to say yes? How do women say "no" when they have said yes enough times before that one more isn't really going to matter? Especially when they have given up all hope of finding something valuable in a man or relationship? Why, in the day of instant gratification, would anyone want to practice restraint? Even though there are still labels for women, the term slut being one of them. Regardless, even though that hypocritical stigma still exists, it is nowhere as strong as it used to be. A woman is not going to be ostracized these days like centuries before. Even decades before.

Here is what is happening, plain and simple, in case you haven't noticed: we, as human beings, need affection. We need connection. We need intimacy. Why else would centuries and centuries of the desire to love and be loved survive through wars and plagues and injustices and death and loss and betrayals and everything this planet has faced since the beginning of time? Love is an innate desire in every single one of us. Now, that may be genetic, manmade, or for the purpose of the procreation of our species. What I do know is that when we deny ourselves this, we deny our very humanity. And when we deny our humanity, the suppression of that desire for love builds up and boils to the point of destruction someplace else.

In this case, in not only denying but also replacing that need with something as superficial as it has become these days, we are the walking malnourished, anorexics of love that are saturated and eaten up by insecurities. Why? Because we have lost our foundational basis in life. We no longer feel secured and anchored in humanity because we deny the very essence of what it is to be human. When you try to ignore something as important as the heart of humanity, then you completely desensitize yourself from it and you use every little distraction there is in this world to make sure you don't ever feel it, hear it calling to you, recollect it. This is where we are today. To be human is to both love and lust, but today we mainly lust. We are a world that has drunk of the technology Kool-Aid. Sex has been sold to us on so many different levels through media and advertising and porn that it does definitely play for team lust, not love. In the vampire obsessed culture we live in sex is the blood needed for survival. If you are trying to be the nice vampire that doesn't feed on and destroy people in order to satisfy that overwhelming hunger, kudos to you. It seems a majority of people see their target, feel the hunger, feed on that target, and then wait until they are hungry again to go on to the next one. They don't realize this until they realize why they are in need, why they are so hungry, they will never be satisfied.

Jackson Square. It is here where the statue of Andrew Jackson stands with the beautiful St. Louis Cathedral (built well before this statue) as the back drop to this monument. Andrew Jackson was the seventh president of The United States and proclaimed hero in the Battle of New Orleans. Jackson square is a beautiful monument and a reminder of the wars fought to bring us to the place we are today. When there is war there is strategy and honor. Or at least there used to be. We are going to take the image of Andrew Jackson on that horse in Jackson Square and delve into the art of war, because we are most certainly at war within.

How does this have anything to do with hooking up? May I present to you the idea of "Counting Coup"? Counting Coup first presented itself in Shakespeare's Hamlet when Hamlet and Laertes engage in a mock fight. Hamlet strikes Laertes with his sword, not enough to wound, and then asks in common terms, "What have you got to say about that?" Meaning, do you acknowledge that, had this been a real fight, I would have just wounded, if not killed, you? Laertes concedes, admitting that yes, indeed, Hamlet had touched him and very well could have injured him. It was a way of fighting without shedding blood or causing harm. Then there are the Indians of North America. Their way of Counting Coup was actually more for prestige and position. Essentially, if they could touch an enemy and escape that enemy unharmed, that was counted as a "coup." The more coups you had, the more respected you were, for you proved your advantage.

Counting Coup was first introduced to me in a conversation I was having with a friend. He had another friend, a very good looking guy, who was trying to maintain some form of restraint in his life when it came to hooking up. He really wanted to find someone he could really connect with and have a relationship with, but he was flailing in the sea of hook-up opportunities always presenting themselves to him. He asked my guy friend for advice. My guy friend told him, "You've got to Count Coup."

How in the world do we, in this day and age, bring some respect back to sex? How do we become more choosy and in doing so give the actual act more value, when there are so many opportunities surrounding us on an everyday basis? You Count Coup. Say what? Count Coup people.

Walk into a bar or party at a friend's house and play a little game with yourself if you have to. Make it a challenge. Realize that Counting Coup is more prestigious than the actual act of "conquering" a person because Counting Coup brings you right to the edge of it, heart beating, here is your opportunity to win, slay, or (in this analogy) lay., Then instead of doing what you know you very well could do, you touch and escape untouched.

Does this make sense to you? Let me break it down in simple terms. You acknowledge in your mind that yes, if you wanted to, you could hook-up with this person you have been playing eye hockey with all night and are now talking to through slurred words and another glass of wine. Yes, you could hook-up with him or her, but instead of doing it, you are going to Count Coup. You are going to "touch" this person with your flirtatiousness and the chemistry and everything else being exchanged between the two of you, but you are going to escape into that cab or out onto that street unscathed. You are going to choose to just acknowledge you could have, but chose not to. Why? Because you are going to have the honor of realizing it takes so much more to refrain than to give in. That is something to be respected.

Counting Coup in Native American times, being able to escape unharmed was the highest honor that could be held. In the analogy of hooking up: to meet someone and to be attracted, to flirt and do your thing, but leave without giving in is the highest honor, much more so than to meet that person, be attracted, and hook-up.

When self-control is practiced, then the very

thing you are maintaining your self-control for, in this case sex, goes up in value. You find it has more worth than you had previously placed on it. As with everything in life that you find valuable, you don't go handing it out to just anyone. Where there is value there is always respect, and where there is respect, there is the highest level of accomplishment. Where there is accomplishment, there is a feeling of pride, and where there is a feeling of pride, there is higher self-esteem. Voilà, you have taken something that has been so defaced and restored it back to its original brilliance. Again, as in everything I have stated thus far, it is not a morality issue. It isn't choosing to not hook-up because you find it morally wrong. Everyone is different when it comes to their beliefs on this. What it is about is choosing not to hook-up because you are tired with the little intimacy fixes you are getting as a faux intimacy junkie. These fixes don't last. They leave you addicted and dependent on the next one in order for you to feel good again. Each time you do this you get further and further away from an actual heartfelt connection to another person.

There is no way to woo a person if you are living life as a pro-athlete in the sport of sex. It just isn't possible. Again, wooing has its roots in respect, value, honor, selectiveness and commitment. Habitual hooking up with people has nothing to do with these things. It is the easy way. That is why the act of Counting Coup in wartime days was such an honor. It took much more skill and discipline than simply conquering a person did.

Wooing takes work. It does.

Counting Coup takes a vigilant effort. And whenever you have a decision to be made, you have to have some form of discipline and focus to make it. That is why a majority of society chooses the easy way, the hook-up way. The non-woo way. I am sure by now that some of the people reading this book might have already put it down, because it takes a certain type of person to take on the Woo Dat challenge. It is not for the weak of heart. It is for the brave of heart.

When Andrew Jackson stepped up to lead the Battle of New Orleans, he made a plan. He impressed the people who were expecting him to be ignorant and "backwoods" by proving he was intelligent and poised. He called upon people, engineers and officials to help show him how best to seal off New Orleans from attack. He sought help from the famous pirate Jean Lafitte. He held off armies twice as big as his army of 3,000. In the end, it was the British who suffered massive losses.

Andrew Jackson could never have accomplished this defeat without a plan. Without focus, without discipline, without doing things differently than most had done before, he never could have succeeded. He was innovative in his strategies and stuck to his guns. He did not back down, rather he lead New

Orleans straight to victory.

Nothing in life is accomplished with ease. You are either a leader of your life, the Andrew Jackson of your life, or you are the one that will be defeated. If you want something great, you have to have it in you to choose something great. Most people, deep down inside, want something great when it comes to a relationship. This does not mean most have something great, however. Statistics show they do not. But how many people take the reins of their own life, strategize, stick to their guns and lead? Not many. Even more, how many people actually have had the realization that this needs to be done in relationships too? Not many.

As if love wasn't difficult enough before, we have the times we are living in that blur the lines and directions that no longer work. It is like using a GPS system that looks up roads and maps from years past that have not been updated. Chances are you are never going to end up at your desired location. And today, if you try and go off of the old ways, it will be the same.

This is why I say bringing the old ways of wooing into the 21st century and mixing both to create a new way of relating is the answer to the dissatisfying way we are living today. Wooing is the strategy. The person you are choosing to woo is the purpose. Every act of woo is the focus, the discipline, the commitment. The outcome is the grandeur felt in the success of victory.

* ● *

How then, can you have any of this if you are randomly hooking up left and right with people? It isn't possible to have both. You are either a sloppy, self-indulging, undisciplined follower or you are a focused, intent, disciplined leader. At the end of the day, it is the leader that reaps the spoils.

To some this may sound like no fun at all. Of course, if you are addicted to the easy way or instant gratification this is going to sound like a buzz kill. That is why not everyone has it in them to create something exceptional. Not everyone was made to be a hero or a leader or to choose evolution as a person. Those who are going around showing zero self-control know nothing different. To them, this is all there is, and the thought of trying to choose anything different sounds boring. But these are not the people I am talking to right now. The person reading this book is tired of the lack of challenge, the bore in the big easy, the shallowness in the hook-up connection. They want something more, something different and that want far exceeds the temporary satisfaction of having every last urge met.

This doesn't apply to everyone, of course. There are those who don't go to bars, who don't meet people in situations where the song "Closing Time" is apropos. But I have seen the same thing happen in coffee shops, the gym, even at the dentist. You meet someone and, depending on where that person or yourself is in the scheme of things, determines the amount of respect brought to the table.

Again, it is not a question of right or wrong. It is a question of what it is you want the outcome to be when you meet a person. If you are tired of the casual and the superficial and want to meet someone you could actually build something with, then you have to change your thinking and ways of relating. If you are a person who is ready for something a little deeper, then you have to break out of the kiddie pool way of connecting with a person.

One way of doing this is by Counting Coup. Show some restraint. Change the habit of giving in and build up some resistance muscle. There are so many people who feel a relationship just isn't desirable anymore. It takes too much work, it's too challenging. That is why hooking up has become the way of fulfilling that need, just in a less meaningful way. But do you think the greats of past times looked at something like going into battle and said..."Nah, that takes too much work"? No, they didn't. Backbone and balls, this is what's missing in today's society. Laziness is taking over. If it takes work, walk away and find what doesn't. If it takes more than the heat of the moment passion needed to connect, then cut the tie and move on to the next one. Whenever challenge presents itself in a connection with another person it is much easier to break it off and disappear. Don't answer that text message or phone call. Turn your back and walk away towards the easy. The easy way means zero confrontation, you owe nothing, a clean break, because you were never truly committed in the first place.

This is why when you woo a person, you have already made the decision that they are worth it. And when you find someone who is worth it, you will gladly work through the challenge. You will do what it takes to discipline yourself. You will build up those lazy love muscles (no pun intended) into something strong enough to carry the connection through to the other side of easy.

How do we begin? Easy, my friends: just start Counting Coup. You do this long enough, it clears the space in your heart and head enough to begin to make the decision about who is worth your woo. Count Coup...the key to woo.

six
Cafe du
Funde'

"Well the coffee is strong at the Cafe Du Monde, and the donuts are too hot to touch; but just like a fool, when those sweet goodies cool, I ate 'til I ate way too much. Cause I'm livin' on things that excite me, be they pastries or lobsters or love; I'm just tryin' to get by being quiet and shy, in a world full of pushin' and shove."

- Jimmy Buffet, The wino and I know.

One of the key components to wooing(and one of the missing components in complacent relationships) is fun. When the fun leaves, happiness leaves. When there is no fun present in things that take commitment, it seems like work and becomes resented. Here's the thing: sometimes fun finds you without you trying. Most times though, you have to plan or create your fun. Most people don't realize this when it comes to relationships. They just expect it to be there, to show up for them without having to do a thing. Then they pout and get bored and distant when fun doesn't come for a visit. They start to blame the relationship or get aggravated with their partner and blame them.

When it comes to wooing, you have to plan fun. Wooing is assertion, remember? It is made up of deliberate acts and gestures. It takes intelligence and creativity. So, if wooing is going to take some effort, why not have some fun with it? Have you ever noticed that the times you are having fun negativity pretty much disappears? How can you be having fun and at the same time hone in on someone's annoying personality traits? How can you be having fun and at the same time thinking, "this is way too much work?" You can't. You can't have fun and complain about anything. They just can't exist in the same moment, unless you are what my friend describes as a "special kind of a-hole."

Cafe Du Monde is the epitome of taking a moment to have fun. If you have never been there, it's a cafe established in 1862. It boasts a gigantic outside patio and waitresses that have been there for decades. Cash only. Besides beignets, coffee, orange juice, and hot chocolate, milk and soda are really the only other items on the menu. Coffee and beignets are what you really come here for.

If you have had a bad day, a busy day, or need to feel five again, you go and sit in the open air cafe and order a beignet. If you are one of the unfortunate souls that have never had the pleasure of biting into a beignet, they are warm, French-style donuts smothered in powdered sugar. If you are lucky, street musicians will be there playing to accompany the slight, involuntary groans coming from you when you bite into one.

I am not sure I have ever sat at a table at Cafe Du Monde and witnessed a couple around me frowning or bored or not talking to each other. I am an observer of people everywhere I go. So, I look for these things. No, most couples are caught smiling or laughing at each other because one of them accidentally snorted powdered sugar up their nose while trying to bite into a beignet and laughing at the same time. It is one of those magical places that you can't help but feel happy in. Unless, of course, you are caught up in one of the long lines waiting for a table. Even then, the anticipation usually outweighs the frustration. Why else would you wait in line for so long?

Apply that to wooing. If you would be willing to wait in line for a plate of warm beignets, why wouldn't you willing to make an effort to woo someone? The end result of both is gratification.

It comes down to priorities. Ever go by a Mac store on the day a new iPhone version came out? How about a concert where people are sleeping out on the sidewalk to be the first in line for tickets or seats? What about Black Friday, where hardworking people will have a sleepless night waiting out in front of stores to be the first one in? What about waking up at the crack of dawn to go fishing? How about being the tenth car in line to get a carwash?

When you want something, you will wait, show up, and commit to doing whatever it takes to get it. The only thing separating you from effort is desire. How strong your desire is determines your willingness and where the object of your desire falls on your list of priorities.

Men, if you are willing to spend money on video games, tee times, overpriced cocktails at a strip club (had to go there) and yet you have never once considered sending flowers to a girl you are interested in, you are simply just being unintelligent. Try doing little things like knowing she wants the new album by her favorite musician. Men, you could have it so much easier than you know, if only you made the woman you are with a priority—like you do these other things. It is not even about "spending money." You know how moved a woman would be if a guy she was into showed up with flowers he picked from her neighbor's front yard on his way down the sidewalk to her house? She would find it clever, daring and even though I am sure her neighbor wouldn't appreciate it...I am more than sure she could get over that. Do you know how she would feel if the guy she is in an actual relationship with took the time to do that? There is nothing she wouldn't do to reciprocate back to him the effort he showed her.

There is nothing that frustrates me more as a

woman than a man (a baiter) who does all of this at the beginning and the moment he feels I am giving in, he lessens it. More to the point, the man that does this and then once he knows he has you in a relationship, acts like the lethargic, couch potato of love. Again, as I said in chapter two, women like a challenge. If they can predict that you are going to do absolutely nothing in the area of romance or wooing, they will get bored and seek it elsewhere. Even if they don't seek it out elsewhere, they will no longer seek anything from you. You will go from sex a few times a week, to once a week, to once every two weeks, to once a month, to once a quarter, to tax day. You know I am speaking truth here.

The same goes for a woman who is intelligent enough to figure out that you are only doing it because you want something and not out of genuine desire (again, a baiter). A woman knows when something that is trying to be special is really that you are the type of man that does this something "special" for a lot of different women when you want to be with them. A woman knows when you are not selective. A woman knows it when you get offended and overly sensitive the moment you don't get your way. How in an instant, all of those acts and gestures stop when you don't get what you want, when you want it, the way you want it. A woman knows your intentions are not on the up and up. She knows when she is something to be captured or used for your needs or insecurities as a man, rather than someone you truly respect and don't "need" to conquer.

Women, do you know how much a man would be moved to do these things for you if you got off of your feminine soap box and finally did something he likes for a change? If you did some research or read a book about how men think or what it is they enjoy instead of just expecting them to be like you?

He comes home from work and you bombard him with questions and conversation. Take the time to learn that sometimes men like to be silent and not have to talk? You drag him out shopping at Bed, Bath, and Beyond, yet you aren't willing to sit through a football game with him. You sit through a football game with him, yet you talk the entire time. You haven't shown one ounce of desire for him all week, yet you expect him not to engage in that 24 year old secretary flirting with him at work or at line at Starbucks?

You tell him for the 20th time to pick up his socks and instead you pick them up and berate him for it over and over again, like a mother, instead of just letting them accumulate. You know what I would do? I would let them become a pile, or if they were all over the room I would simply pick them up and toss them into a pile. After the socks made a mound, I would make a handwritten sign and glue it to a Popsicle stick. The sign might say something like "Mt. Sockerest." Instead of nagging, making a point in a fun way will get you way better results.

Most women, however, would never even think of letting the socks pile up, much less how to go about it in a way a man would appreciate. No way. Men are supposed to just get it and be like us, the idiots! Right? You keep thinking that way and getting the same results every time. Einstein said this: "Insanity is doing the same thing over and over again and expecting different results." Even though men throw around the term crazy about women simply because it means they couldn't understand their emotional state, actually living out the quote above is about the only time where crazy is genuinely called for.

Women, it is not being submissive or repressed or giving in if you simply learn how to communicate best with men. Like diplomacy, diplomats must use the right tactics to get what they want. Life is one big negotiation. How else do you get through it when you have so many different personalities, beliefs and agendas? If you learn that as long as you keep it fun, you will get way farther ahead in the communication. I fail at this all the time, I do. I will even go so far as to say I have just recently realized, since writing this book, that my trying to express my feelings and having to write that mile long email, and trying over and over to fix it through words and long conversations...that this is equivalent to me beating myself with a dead horse. I get nowhere, and although it helps me as a woman to release what I am feeling, I do not get the end result I am hoping for.

If you want to build something with the person you are interested in, if you want to maintain a fire in that relationship you have built, if you want to stay with a person that you feel you are in love with, you will woo. You will woo from the beginning until the end, taking the time to know what that person thinks wooing is. Taking the time to do things they like and enjoy even when they are not your preferences, is wooing. Making an effort to do things for that person in the same way you will make an effort for the other things you want in life is wooing.

You must have some integrity to do this though. Your actions have to be truthful and based on truly respecting a person, not doing it for the sake of some insecure need inside you that just has to have that person. This is the mistake so many make. We chase and chase and chase and when we get it, that desire is gone. This is the #1 red flag indicating whether or not you are woo worthy or the person you are pursuing is woo worthy. Like anything else, it will take a conscious decision to continue to woo, but it will not dissipate like an apparition in front of you the moment there is a challenge or lack of challenge because you have now gotten what you want.

There is such a fine line between the true woo and the woo used for gain. It is almost so fine that it is difficult to point out and explain here. The only way I can describe it is to break it down for each gender.

For women it is the feeling you get when a man is coming on hot and heavy with his pursuit and you can sense it is not genuine or for you alone. It is for the prize that he has made you in his mind. For men it is when you have the type of girl that shows signs of not really being interested in who you really are. If you already, at the beginning, have to be something you are not or hide your thoughts so you don't scare her off or cause an argument. If you are with a girl who seems to always take but never offers to give in return yet shows no signs of really wanting to move forward with you. The ones who let you pay over and over and never pick up a tab. The ones that call you up and ask you to meet them out, but oh, by the way, they have invited a couple girlfriends along too and expect you to pay the tabs the whole night. This is crossing that fine line.

The reason it's a fine line is because wooing is always done for an end result. It just takes a person getting to the point where they woo like they would anything else they want to take care of in their lives. You plant a garden? You show up and water that garden. You do what it takes to attend to it. You get a new car? You take the time to wash it and keep it clean. You get that new gym membership? You take time out of your day to make use of it and show up and work out. You have a good job? You show up every day and you do it, hopefully to the best of your ability. All of these things have an end result though.

Your garden grows. Your car is clean and shiny. Your body is in shape. You get paid on pay day.

If you are wooing for honorable reasons, you will understand that it is not a one-time thing. It is not to be done only until you get what you want. It is not to be done for every person you meet and find attractive. It is selective and long term because you want it to go somewhere, to grow, to stick around for all time. If this is where you are coming from, you will want to make it something enjoyable and fun while you do it.

Whether you are wooing in the beginning or wooing in an established relationship, you will make a conscious effort to have fun doing it. Just like when people take the time out of their day to go and sit at Cafe Du Monde and enjoy something sweet and delicious, we have to take the time in our day to do the same, to plan a Cafe Du Funde'. Fun is the quintessence of romance. Men, if you will realize this, that romance can be fun, it won't seem like the kryptonite to fun. Women, if you will do this for yourself every day instead of waiting for a man to come along and do it, you may find that romance is the very thing you extract out of that man.

The problem with most people is they get high off the fumes of beginning love endorphins and then when those fade, well, they stop feeling high. That is why it is absolutely necessary to set the pace out of the gate. Have fun from the beginning. Make days of fun. Moments of fun. Make it your goal to be the gold medalist of fun, the world record holder, the expert.

To me, it makes total and complete sense to take the obvious and mold it as if it were play-doh into the shape and image of what it is you want. In this case, there are two obvious elephants in the room. Number one: if you are going to commit to wooing someone it is going to take effort. I have now said that at least ten times. Make the effort fun and it won't feel like exertion. Again, as excited as you feel waiting in line for that iPhone or Jimmy Choo shoe, is how excited you should feel when you do an act of woo. Make it fun. Number two: it is a scientific fact that the longer you stay with a person, the more the passion wanes. It waxes and it wanes. Just like the moon. It's human nature. It's like that new car smell. Can you ever pinpoint exactly the date after you buy a new car that you can't smell it anymore? Nope. What happened? Did the smell go away or did your olfactory system just go on strike saying, "Been there, smelled that?" During the times you are feeling it less, try doing something fun with your significant other. It will bring it back. Life gets in the way of fun sometimes.

Unfortunately, there are way more stressful and every day boring moments than fun ones. So, if when you are in a passion rut and you go out and do something fun it brings back that feeling. Just like when you leave your car for an extended period of time and come back to it and get a whiff of that "new car smell." The problem is, most couples get into that rut and the last thing they want to do is have fun. Most want to wallow in the misery and then through either a look that could kill or a passive aggressive comment, they will make a point to blame the other for making them wallow in it.

Funday. This is what you want to plan when it comes to wooing. No matter if you are just starting out with a person or if you have been with them for a while. In your mind, visit Cafe Du Funde' and make a plan for as many fun things as you can think of doing. Of course, don't make the planning of these fun things feel like work. Let it be easy.

Wooing is fun. Watching the one you are wooing laugh and be happy is proof of that.

So, that gym schedule you are on or tee time you have once a week or yoga class or pole dancing class or TV show you just have to watch or set your DVR for? If you can set time for these things, you can set time for Cafe Du Funde'.

seven
Woodoo

"Marie Laveau was one of the kindest women who ever lived, and one who probably did more good to a great number of people here than any other who lived to her great age."

—The City Item

Marie Laveau, the great Voodoo Queen of New Orleans. There is much more speculation than there are known facts about her. One thing is certain: she was powerful. A hairdresser, healer, and mother of 15 children. She was a devout Catholic. She was respected and feared. She was said to be a shrewd business woman. She was said to be a woman who took in anyone who was hungry, hurting, or sick. She nursed men and women alike who had contracted yellow fever and were most certainly on their deathbeds, yet somehow they miraculously escaped their fates.

The Voodoo of today has become polluted and

marred with rumor and assumption and as with any religion, abuses of power. The one thing we are going to focus on here is the one thread that runs through Voodoo that doesn't need to frighten anyone, no matter what your beliefs are. That thread is the act of ritual. The whole religion is based on ritual. And I am not talking about sacrificing chickens here. I'm talking about something as simple as lighting a specifically colored candle for a specific need or prayer. Every religion has this. Whether it is prayer, going to church, going on specific days, celebrating religious holidays. Even football fans have this. Anything that is habitual for respect or reverence(?).

Wooing takes acts of sacrifice. Again, not talking about chickens here. Anything that takes thought, time, and execution is sacrifice. You are sacrificing little and/or big things. Like time. You might look like a fool, so you sacrifice your pride. It might cost something, so you sacrifice your hard earned money. It might make you vulnerable, so you sacrifice your guard.

To woo is to create an act of romance and/or appreciation. The word "woo" is a verb, an action. Little, mini-rituals performed for something you want, something that makes your heart happy, something that excites you. It floors me that people can paint their faces on any given Sunday and stand in the freezing cold or rain to root on their football team but they can't make the effort to make their partner feel special. Kind of sad, isn't it? Priorities are askew, people.

If you take the most basic Voodoo ritual there is setting up an altar might come to mind. Buying specific offerings for the specific Deity you pray to, whether that is candy or flowers or in some cases rum or a cigarette. I am positive there have been people on this planet that have tried a prayer or two and have run around town buying candles and rum thinking, "What the hell am I doing?", yet they do it anyway (depending on how committed they are to their prayer). Prayer is intent. You have an intent, you show up for that intent and do whatever it takes to show you are present, willing, open, desiring, needing, wanting, asking.

Not into football and Voodoo weirds you out? Let's go back to standing in line for your latest iPhone fix. Let's go back to spending your weekly paycheck on a pair of Christian Louboutin shoes, knowing you are going to be eating Ramen Noodles until you get paid again. Lent is a good example of sacrifice for a belief in the act of fasting. Every religion has its prayers and customs and holidays to celebrate or observe a tradition. It is part of our human makeup and has been since the beginning of time.

Let me just ask some simple questions. Why would you take something as sacred as love and maintain the belief that you have to do nothing for it other than spend thousands on a wedding where you say a few vows? Why would you meet someone you are interested in and not start out of the gate on your best foot? Why would you buy into the belief that love will take care of itself and if it doesn't, well then, it wasn't meant to be...and on to the next person? Why would you do something as important as connecting your life with someone else's and yet never take the time to ever truly know them? You just show up every day playing by the "rules" set for each of the sexes, never questioning them. Never wondering if there is a better way that might get better results? Never wondering if maybe we have it all wrong?

Statistics in relationships generally suggest we are on the wrong track. According to the United States Census Bureau, over 44% of the American population is single. That is over 100 million people!

It's kind of shocking, when you take a step back and look at it all. As a society, we have become so lazy. We have become slackers, unmotivated by anything other than quick pleasure. We have become a society of self-focused people. And when you are self-focused you don't see anything in front of you. You trip up, you have no vision. You only focus on what you need. This makes relationships in general difficult.

A person who is willing to woo, is a person who has gotten over a lot of their general hang-ups. Hang-ups like: the fear of rejection, the expectation of something in return, presenting yourself to be something you really are not. Hang-ups like the neediness associated with using people to fill a void because you have a gaping sinkhole swallowing up one you-must-be–the-one-for-me" person at a time. I can spot those men instantly. I see them walking toward me and I just want to hold up a sign that says "I'm not your Queen, move on." That may sound harsh, but you know the kind I am talking about.

Men or women that look at you as if you are the one for them after knowing you for five minutes, may want to crown you their king or queen. After you show no interest, they get pissy and then it happens with the next quasi-attractive person they meet. I actually understand their plight, because that can happen and does. But the ones I am speaking of go from person to person thinking the same thing about each of them. Something in them is a romantic at heart. They just haven't done the work to at least hone in a bit on what it is they really want to have in a person. Their loneliness or need takes over and is that aggressive energy you feel when you first meet them, which is a total turn-off. Wooing from this place will get you nowhere.

So let's say you are all cleaned up or at least getting there. You have made yourself Woo worthy. You have recognized the Master Daters and The Master Baiters. You see that WOOwolf dressed up like grandma and you pass on the basket of goodies. My, what a fast text messenger you are grandma!

The sexy Jean Laffite-like bad boy or girl tried to get their hooks in you last night and you actually found it unattractive. You are adding to your numbers, Counting Coup that is. You have made it a habit to have Cafe Du Funde's, not just with someone else, but solo too. And you are now asking, "How the hell do I woo someone?" I'm so glad you asked.

We are going to cover it all here. Wooing someone you just met. Wooing someone you are in a relationship with. Wooing someone you are not only in a relationship with, but also living with. Wooing someone in business. Wooing someone in your family. We are going to put the woo all over you. In every single connection you have.

Let's get started. Say you just met someone and really clicked in a way that is truly unique. You don't have to think too much into it or attach a white picket fence and two-car garage to it. You just trust the instinct that this is a little different than the other connections you have made. Let's say (guys) that you get the girl's number. Or maybe it didn't even get to that and she said, "Find me on Facebook." I cringe at that, but it happens. This stupid three day rule thing...you know what I think about it? If a guy waits three days to call me or contact me then I am already turned off. Why? Because he just proved he is not an individual. He is someone who read or heard somewhere that you should wait three days and so I know already that he is not the kind of guy I would be interested in. Why? Because being an individual is one of the things I have identified as a character trait I admire in a person.

Several years ago I met a guy through mutual friends. I wasn't interested in him on a romantic level per se, but knew we would be friends and we had similar businesses, so I felt it would be a beneficial connection for us both. He asked for my number, I gave it and left. I wasn't even to my car before he text messaged me something along the lines of "Great meeting you! P.S. I follow the three minute rule." I thought it was funny and clever.

My best friend has this saying and I'm pretty sure it is not her own, but it asserts that "you can never say the wrong thing to the right person. You can never say the right thing to the wrong person." Pretty elementary, but in all things there has to be balance. Too much of something is never a good thing. That guy's text to me made me laugh. He wasn't overbearing. In fact, we exchanged maybe two more texts after that and that was it. But I didn't cross him off the list because he contacted me right away or didn't wait three days.

When it comes to being asked out on a date though, the good old-fashioned phone call is the best. Act one of wooing. In this day and age, it is a "wow" factor when someone picks up the phone to make those initial plans. I know text messaging is easier on so many levels. The rejection (if there is going to be any) is easier. It doesn't put the person you are asking on the. It is more comfortable. I get all of that. Again though, if someone risks all these things and shows enough effort to make a phone call to ask you out on a date, it automatically shows he thinks enough about you to take the time and risk to do it. I know we are in the year 2013 and girls ask guys out all the time and the same thing applies. It shows bravery and guts to call a guy and ask him to that hockey game. He will be impressed. let's ask a few more simple questions.

Why would you approach a date like you would a friend you are asking to meet you at the park? There has to be some awe to it or it isn't special. Add a sprinkle of awe. Pick up the damn phone and dial. You are setting the precedent for the way the rest of the connection will unfold from that point on. If the person you are asking finds that odd or "creepy" (the favorite word used today), then they are not Woo Worthy and you got your answer at the very beginning instead of well into it.

I just heard an excellent story about a guy who wanted to ask a girl out. He knew her through friends, so he knew where she lived. He got thick paper, like photographers use for backdrops, and on one side of the paper he wrote how he would like to take her out on a date. That part was on the backside. He taped the paper to the door and actually cut it out to be the whole size of the door to her house. On the front he put "WARNING: Asbestos Removal!!!" She got home and was stunned; laughed her head off. She said it was taped on so well she couldn't just pull it off. She had to actually run through it like a football player. Needless to say, he got the date.

Are you getting the picture?

Girls, you have a guy at work that you get along great with? You're friends and flirt and you wish he would ask you out. He's shy. Maybe he doesn't think he has a chance in the world that you might say yes. You find out he loves baseball? You don't have a professional baseball team in your city. Find out where the local pee wee baseball team plays. Hand draw with crayons or markers tickets to their next game. Leave them on his desk. When he says, "That was funny! Let's do it!" Take two hotdogs, or veggie dogs (whatever you eat). Boil them or grill them. Cut them in pieces. Put them in a Tupperware bowl. Add ketchup, mustard and relish. Toss the hotdogs around in it. Bring a box of toothpicks. Enjoy your little hotdog treats while you watch the little pee wee team play their little pee wee hearts out. Now that is a clever first date. That is wooing. Not only were you creative, but you took initiative. You took something you have learned he loves. You put forth effort and time to make it special. It might not turn into a relationship, but I guarantee you he will remember that date all his life and so will you.

Say you are a texter. You just love to text. I like

to text, nothing wrong with that. Here's an idea: after you have made that first phone call to ask someone out, make it fun. Tell that person you want to take them on a date in seven days. Only, at the end of seven days, you want to know seven new things about them. Tell them they have to text you something new every day that is a fun little fact about them. And you have to do the same. Make sure you incorporate one of the things you learn about the person in your date come the 7th day. Wooing. It is that simple. Making someone wait seven days is only going to add to the mystique, which will only add to the passion and excitement of it. Make sense?

Let's move on to the person you have been dating. So many couples start dating and the intensity of pursuit wares off. This is normal to an extent. However, it is also a choice. Most people stop choosing to romance and woo their lover. Laziness creeps in, complacency. If there are other things in your life, be it your job, or attainment of material things, etc., that you show up for and continue to do what it takes to maintain upkeep of that thing and yet, you don't do this for your partner? It is so simple for men and yet they make it so complex. To say women are complicated and to have the belief that women are impossible to figure out are just excuses. Rubik's Cubes are complicated and still manage to get "figured out".

Women feel the same way about men too. It

is only the laziness both men and women have that keeps them from trying to learn about the opposite sex. It's like people from different cultures thinking they will one day understand what it feels like to come from another place. There is no way. You can learn, experience it for yourself, but you will never truly know or be like that culture. With this said, it is simple to understand what turns a woman on when it comes to a relationship. Effort on the man's part, period. Show me you still desire me. Show me you still want to pursue me, if not for the sake of making sure that every day I choose *you*. Show me you don't automatically think you have it in the bag and somehow own me. Show me you actually took the time to do something. Show me it is still me you want, even though I know every day you could make the choice otherwise. This is what turns a woman on. It isn't about money or power. It is as simple as picking some flowers on the side of the road. What does that cost you? 60 seconds of your time? A woman wants to feel pursued throughout the courtship and relationship.

In fact, the relationship should be a never-ending courtship. It is what keeps the passion alive, the excitement in the relationship. It keeps the appreciation and gratitude from becoming stagnant. It is what all women want.

Women, when it comes to men, they want almost the same. They want to see the awe and desire in your eyes that you had the moment you met and became attracted to them, that look that says, "You can do no wrong". That adoration that is so easily destroyed through nagging and being disappointed and "mothering" that comes over a lot of women further into a relationship.

Have you ever experienced finding out that a man was cheating on some woman you know and the woman he is cheating on is stunning? You see the woman he is cheating with and she's not even close to as attractive? What's that about? Adoration, plain and simple. Men have egos. You will never change that or nag it out of them. They need constant praise. It's true. That is their language. They don't, however, want a doormat and that is not what I am talking about here. It is about the choice to--in every day you are with someone--see them through new eyes. Not the eyes that only notice their flaws.

The part of women that can multitask, remember conversations, actually think of the consequences before doing something, it's these missing attributes of men that women can't handle. When a man lacks these qualities the disappointment and aggravation starts to fester in a woman. That sharp tone, that disappointed look in your eye, the way you withhold because you are so turned off by his "stupidity" or lack of "spine" this is what chips away, bit by bit, the man you once fell in love with.

So what came first? The only absolute in all of

this is that the one thing that can be changed is your choice about how you relate. This is where wooing separates the weak hearts from the brave hearts. If you don't want to take the time, if it seems like too much work, if you are ok and happy with being miserable, or if you convince yourself that the changes and space growing in between the two of you is acceptable--then you choose not to woo. It's that simple.

Some acts of wooing the one you love include the following: Say your guy or girl is really looking forward to their favorite band's new album that is about to be released. You have heard them mention it. Buy them concert tickets or the CD. So simple, yet so thoughtful. How about you both take a day off of work? Yep, I am suggesting you call in sick, love sick. Stay in bed all day and just be lazy. Order one movie after the other. Order pizza or Chinese food. Drink wine in bed. Have a lazy day of doing nothing but loving, enjoying and being with each other.

Say your girl loves roses, but you don't even think to surprise her by sending flowers unless it is that dreaded V-day. Go online and find an essential oil website. Buy an empty vial ($1.50), buy rose oil (anywhere from $15-100+), fill the empty vial with the oil, tell her you made it for her. She will melt. It might take you 10 minutes to order it and pour it. The effort does not even compare to the adoration you will receive. Something as simple as taking it from its bottle and pouring it into an empty one is the magic that a woman will go nuts over. That little bit of ridiculous effort that you, as a man, would never even give thought to or could care less about.

Women, do your men love to golf? Have you never played, don't know how, don't care? Surprise your man with a tee time, drive the cart and be a caddy for the day. Join him. Find out and actually care about what he enjoys. That, of course, doesn't mean you should crash his golf time at every opportunity. How about football? You don't like it? Surprise him one game day with beer and chicken wings and watch a game with him. Don't yap all the way through it. But do ask him, during commercial breaks to explain things you don't understand about the game. Just take a minute to learn what he finds fun and important. That is not being weak or submissive. That is being a friend--which women all too often are not to the men in their lives. Don't be a mother, he already has one. Be a friend.

You live together? Create a "love alter", this can be as simple as a tabletop or fireplace mantle in your bedroom. Add candles or things that remind you of love. It doesn't have to be girly or make your guy think, "holy puke fest!" It just needs to be fun. Leave little hand written post-it notes for each other. Leave a $5 bill on the alter to treat your significant other to his/her Starbucks of the day. Have it be a place where you both get excited to walk by and look at because there might be a surprise or gift on it! Don't leave something every day or it can lose its specialness. Just make sure you maintain it with surprises and well... love.

Say you don't have time in the morning to make your partner breakfast? Take a night to take a muffin pan. Fill it with eggs, bacon, cheese, spinach... whatever you like. Bake it. Take it out. Remove the muffin like mini- casseroles and put them in individual plastic bags and freeze them. Wake up, go pee, brush your teeth, hopefully wash your hands...and go into the kitchen and pop one of those in the microwave while your girl/guy gets ready for work. They walk into the kitchen after and there is their coffee or juice and breakfast. Simple but thoughtful.

How about a business relationship? Whether it's a partnership or a client or someone you want to sell a product or service to, woo them. Find out what they like that would allow them to feel appreciated. Keep the gratitude and appreciation alive with little acts of thoughtfulness. It goes a long way in building partnerships with people. No, it is not bribing or trying to buy someone. I am not just talking about monetary things here. It can be as simple as going to the coffee pot and taking the last bit of coffee left and knowing that your co-worker or business partner will want some coffee later. You take the time to make a fresh pot. There are so many ways to make someone feel appreciated and special. These are ways to keep the respect in business transactions that, when missing, often turns them into resentful relationships, which they all too often do.

Woodoo: small acts of love and appreciation. Rituals in the form of pursuing and showing someone you want them in your life on a daily basis, and not taking that fact for granted. No matter what your belief, if you will take a moment out of your 24 hour day to think a good thought of that person it will do them wonders. Just say "thank you" in your head for that person in your life. Wish them well or think good thoughts for them. These are prayers. Even if you don't believe in praying. Good thoughts or good vibes do have an effect on people. This is woodoo.

I could give idea after idea, example after example, but if you do not feel the desire to make the choice to woo, it will not happen. Wooing is for the people who are on the edge--people who are teetering back and forth, knowing they are not quite happy, but not necessarily knowing how to change that.

I spoke to a young woman yesterday and in the conversation, as I have had with many girls in their 20's, she revealed to me that she had never met a guy that actually took her on a date. Can you believe that? It was always being out somewhere and texting each other and meeting up while with their friends. This generation doesn't even know what it means to woo. They have no clue.

* ● *

The only weed I see that is choking out romance in this world is selfishness. Selfishness perpetuated by the self-absorbed world we live in based on the technology we fill every moment of every day with. I couldn't even start to pinpoint where it has all gone off course. I guess we could start with the child or adolescent who, instead of going outside and playing or taking a walk, is inside all day long, eyes glued on a TV screen as they play video games for hours. It starts with the parents who never connect with their children because they can't get the child's attention off the games or the phone or the computer. This is the beginning of a generation that doesn't know how to connect with something that isn't in HD.

That is why rituals are so much a part of the art of wooing. They make you focus on something outside of yourself, get off of that computer, put that phone down. They make you want to please someone other than yourself. They cause you to remember what it feels like to give and commit to something, to do something for the sake of showing affection rather than getting something in return. They align you back with that part of yourself that wants to give as much as you get. That is in every one of us. It happens at Christmas time or birthdays when you gift someone you love so much and you are just happy watching them open it, just as excited about them opening it as you would be if you were the one actually getting a gift. We all want to give and when we don't, we don't feel good inside.

Selfishness is like a cancer. It takes over and before you know it, selfishness is all there is. Unless you make the choice to practice giving. Practice wooing through the rituals of giving, thoughtfulness, appreciation and romance.

The key to wooing starts with a choice. You have to make the choice first. Commit to practicing Woodoo. You have to make the choice every day. The choice that in some way, you are going to say or do something that allows that other person to know you want them. It is your offering to them, every day. The offering that asks, "Will you please share my life with me today?" And the gratitude through an act of woo that says, "Thank you, for sharing another day with me."

Woo Dat!

eight
The Return
of The Woo

I know the quote above may be brutal but hey,
Anthony Bourdain can be brutally honest, it's part of
what I like about him. The similarity in that quote to
the state of heart-felt-love-relationships of today is
more to the point.

Love is like New Orleans. It is a seasoned and
old soul. It's magical and either takes you in with
all it has, or really f's you up. It has countless fallen
hearts on its battlefield. The wounded, the dead and
the victorious. There's no prejudice, they all walked
and fought on these grounds. It has gone through
countless stages and faces. It shows up disguised

as many things, but it is always love underneath the masks. Like Mardi Gras, there is great pleasure and indulgence in love. Like Mardi Gras, there is always a mess to clean up after such indulgences. Love is art, it is music, and it is food that fills you up and satisfies you to the bones, only to leave you hungry again. Yes, love is like New Orleans.

Like New Orleans, love has been dealt a major blow. A catastrophe of sorts that has left it demolished and only those who truly, genuinely serve it and love it are the ones left to go through the debris and rebuild it back to its former glory. Just like New Orleans, it will never be as it once was. It is impossible,. Maybe it's not meant to be. With the sacred preservation of what is left of the old, the new can be allowed in and a new kind of energy can begin. An alchemy that is not necessarily better, but inevitable.

Is it fixable? I certainly hope so, otherwise I just spent an enormous amount of time writing this book birthed in Crescent City. The question is not whether it is fixable, rather if there is anyone out there that finds it worth fixing. If enough of society has never known what it was like before this technological hurricane than it will be lost forever. Fables and folklore and something written in books found in the few 2nd hand shops that Kindle, Nook and ipad haven't put out of business.

WOO DAT is not so much a how-to as it is a call to arms. If there is any part of you that feels a loss, a part of you that remembers feeling something deeper that really doesn't exist anymore. If there's a part of you that can't quite put your finger on it, but knows that something is amiss; this is a call for you to do something about it. It starts with you. It starts with me. It starts with taking responsibility, not disappearing at the first sign of growing pains. The decision is yours to take the controls of this runaway train and get it back on track again.

All those video games, all those heroes created in Vampire movies and trilogies, all the real life battles happening on this planet that "other people" fight... this is battle happening right in your own home. That home being your heart, your head and your body. You are the only person that can stand up and do what it takes to defend that ground.

That may sound like an overly serious or overwhelming, "let someone else handle it" kind of scenario. The problem is, just like in New Orleans, there is no one else that is going to handle it. Only the people who are willing to stay, willing to sacrifice, willing to hold on, willing to work through, willing to remember, willing to fight, willing to believe, willing to sweat, willing to cry, willing to stand, willing to join each other, willing to take action, willing to rebuild brick by brick, step by step are the ones that will invoke changes.

This is a call to arms where wooing is your big gun. That's right, rebuilding "connection" one woo act at a time. Whether that is romantic, friendly, business, or familial. The commitment to wooing is that stand needed, that sacrifice given, that action taken to dig deeper. To not forget to acknowledge intimacy in connections as much as you acknowledge the ease of technology in connections today. It's about going back to the start, where allowing the heart to be open and unblocked meant feeling magic, pain, pleasure and something deeper than we allow ourselves to feel in the year 2013. It is congestive heart failure-- in the emotional sense-- that is the leading cause of death of all that is intimate in the digital age.

The human heart, the "emotional" heart, is akin to those old shuttered doors you see when walking through the French Quarter, bolted up. No light gets in. Grand courtyards and archways, crown molding and hardwood floors, fireplaces and mantles, claw foot bathtubs and pedestal sinks, shut up tight for no one to see. No human touch, no human voice, no footsteps to be heard. No hands to touch the wooden banister railings of the spiraling staircases. No one to witness what was once glorious and thriving. Dust accumulates. Chandeliers hang with no electricity to make them shine. Paint chips and walls decay. Where once music filled rooms and traveled out open doors to balconies onto the streets, now there is only silence. Yes, boarded shutters nailed shut and forgotten, this is what has happened to the "heart" of communication.

* ● *

It takes someone coming along who has the means to unbolt those shutters and let the light in. Someone who will not be overwhelmed by the amount of work it will take to restore, but who be moved with excitement and passion to create something marvelous out of something destitute. Do you have the means to do this for your own heart? Do you even see the value in that? These are the questions that determine whether you are one who is going to stand up and fight.

If I can do it, anyone can do it. Mistakes are made, you get off track, you lose time, get wrapped up in the very things discussed in these pages. I have done it. Most people have. It doesn't mean that today something new can't be chosen. Only it takes the choice and a commitment to that choice.

One night, I was crossing Bourbon Street to get back to my hotel, in stilettos. Yes, dumb of me, I know. My heel got caught in one of the cracks in the street and well, my shoe stayed and I tumbled forward, falling to my knees. I scraped my knee and joked around by calling it scurvy knee. It seemed like it took forever to heal. Around that time, I had a situation that caused me some pain, emotionally. Nothing serious, just another scraped knee. There was some silent expectation--whether on my part or maybe from what I sensed from others) that it should just be something I got over with in a snap of my fingers. Done. Over. Let it go. Move on. I remember staring down at me knee during that time and thinking, "but my knee hasn't even healed...how can I expect my heart to be?"

This is what we do to ourselves and others. We don't give adequate attention or time to our hearts for feeling, processing, and healing. I ignored my knee, like I tried to ignore my heart at that time. I still have a scar.

Wooing is a return to allowing the heart to live in the light. Not closed off, but open. Giving it the chance to integrate back into communication with logic. A state where they can live as allies, not as opposing forces trying to obliterate the other. Why is wooing this important to the survival of love and the heart? You can say things all day long, you can think things all day long, but until they are backed up with action, they don't really exist. They are brought into physical manifestation through action and action alone. To even form an action, you have to have a commitment to that action. Your hand, your heart, your head, your faith, all of it has to commit to that action in order to even fulfill it. Wooing is action. If love and physical attraction, camaraderie and friendship, hopes, dreams, romance, if even one of these is present, it takes action to bring it to life. Otherwise, it is just a dream.

Getting back to these simple things, putting a plug in the consequences of the more destructive, selfish behavior--this is enough to help get us back on track and saving intimate connections from being something on the extinction list. I've made the choice. I hope by doing that in my own life, it will have a ripple effect throughout every other life I cross. Then it will go on to work through their lives and then the lives of the people they know, and so on. That is the answer to the overwhelming feeling that you are **just** one person and the inadequacy to invoke change that can follow.

Wooing, however, is just the medicine needed, whereas the ailment needs to be addressed first. Diagnosed. Attended to. That is difficult. To pinpoint one thing that is the root of all we are experiencing in our culture today on the subjects of love and communication. If I had to pinpoint it right now, like the world was going to explode or hazelnut chocolate was going to be taken away from me for life unless I do, I would have to say the aliment is fear of commitment. Disdain for commitment. A newfound absolute dislike of the word, its meaning or anything having to do with it. Technology, though it has its wonderful benefits, has enabled this to be. We live in a day and age where we can't focus on any one thing for an extended period of time. Instant gratification is the name of the game now. Everything is about speed and time. New ways to cook things faster. No waiting line. No waiting for internet connection. Everything is expedited. We have zero patience or tolerance for anything that takes time.

* * *

If this is the case in our everyday living, it will be the case in our relationships. Across the board in life. Think of how many you know, and you could be one of them, that has difficulty sitting and reading a book or even an article without being distracted. Think about how annoyed you become when you have to wait for something. Think about how excited you become with the showtime tap dance that you are fed with every single gadget and advertisement there is out there today. This is the culprit. If I had to choose something. No one wants to commit anymore.

You see, this permeates into our ways of thinking and believing. Into our desires. Believe it or not, this isn't a new thing. If you want to go back to the basics, a lot of men woo simply to conquer. It is an ego driven deed. Once that woman is theirs...once she gives in... once she is captured, she becomes very real. Once that ego is satisfied, it becomes real and very scary to men. What is so scary? Commitment. That is when you see them flee. You never hear from them again. That is when, men, you don't reply back. You don't give another thought. You are through and already gone.

A lot of women woo for the sake of manipulation. To get what they want from men. They will lead on and take whatever is offered. They will play the game and the moment they have what they want or someone new comes along that is willing to give it to them, that is when they no longer want to receive from you. That is when you will hear the words she has never spoken in all the time you have been taking her to dinner and surprising her with nice things. You will hear the "it's not you, it's me" speech and she will take off, out of your life faster than your favorite sports car. What is she afraid of? She also is afraid of commitment. Commitment to a man she knows she is only using. This is one of the ways that women need to come clean.

The wooing I speak of in this book is based on inner integrity. It is not about attaining something that is only a fix to you. Your next "it" thing. That thing you will wear out and throw away the moment you are bored and ready for the next new thing. The woo I speak of comes from a man who is honest with himself and has character and from a woman who is honest with herself and has character. You don't have to be perfect...you just have to get real.

Men, we really aren't as difficult to figure out as you make us to be. I will let you in on a big secret, one that really is the root of the reactions that women give you that sometimes leave you scratching your head in complete bafflement. If you have been dating, living with or married to a woman for an extended period of time, her aggravations and knee jerk reactions to you aren't about the fact that you forgot to take the trash out or you space out or you threw your socks down on the floor again. No, that does frustrate women, but not enough for that "if looks could kill" and later

"I've got a headache" type of reaction. I will tell you why your woman has an underlined aura of pissed off-ness. It is because you have changed. Period. It happens in every single relationship. Very few men have been let in on this little secret, so very few men have actually been smart enough to change it so they invoke a happy and loving response from their other half.

How have you changed, you might be asking? You stopped wooing. Plain and simple. You aren't as attentive as you were when you were first pursuing. No, in fact, you have become quite lazy. You stopped "acting" as if you would do anything in the world for her. Here is an absolute fact about all women, although it comes in varying degrees: every woman has a sixth sense. An intuition. She felt that driving force in you, that passion at the beginning that made her feel so wanted. As if she were this grand prize you would do anything to win. Just as she sensed that at the beginning, she also senses the moment that wanes in you because the hunt is over. Instead of her simply calling you on it...she lets it build up. Resentment after resentment. You know that thing called jealousy? When she sees you checking out some other woman? It isn't about the fact that you desire the other woman. It is the fact that you don't look at her that way anymore. She senses in the moment you are looking at the chic at the other table, what you used to do when you looked at her and it reminds her you don't do that anymore.

This is where men have made a major faux pas when it comes to the tradition of wooing. You somehow have convinced yourself it is only until you "capture." Well, that is true if you are going to throw what you caught back out into the wild or devour it once. If you intend on keeping it around, you better keep wooing. This is the language of women. This is what women are starving for from their men. It is so simple. It just takes a little effort and discipline on your part. The same way you make effort keeping your car maintained. The same way you get excited and watch your favorite sports. The same way you show up for your job every day. So much headache could be obliterated from your world if you would just make this simple change. That is literal! If you would keep wooing, you most likely wouldn't here her give you the excuse that she has a headache. In fact, even if she did have one, she would go for it. It is the 100% natural aphrodisiac turn on for a woman. When a man, after getting what he wants, still woos. Don't believe me? Try it.

You can start your first act of woo today by starting the WOO DAT CHALLENGE. It only takes finishing this book and when you do, think of that person you know that might need this or benefit from it, or find it interesting or even find it amusing and make fun of it. Gift this book to that person. That is your first act of woo. You thought about who might like this and you gave it to them. That simple!

I am not alone in this and neither are you. Every person I have spoken to concerning the contents of this book has asked immediately "When and where can I get it?". There are many people out there feeling the same way. Maybe not quite sure of what it is or what to do it about it, but knowing there is some truth to the fact that every day that passes, there is something being lost. Even if we don't know what exactly that "something" is.

Through the points mentioned in these chapters, you can at least find your way and regain your footing enough to stand, though it is different for everyone. No one has the same story or emotional or logical make-up. No one has the same beliefs or upbringing. Some might be similar, but not exact. So the things mentioned in this book are there to help at least stop the current enough for you to get out of it. From there, it is you that creates your woo story and they will be different for each and every one of us.

Just like the quote that started this chapter, deeper communication and love may be maimed and on its last leg, but it is not dead. Not by any means. It just takes being able to look at it in its current state and still see the beauty it once held and the choice to bring that beauty back again, one act of woo at a time.

Are you ready for the return of the woo? Are you going to be part of the movement or just watch as it happens around you? Are you ready to stand for something that really counts? Are you ready to be a real-life super hero of love? I know I am! I hope you are too. Bringing back the old school way of wooing into the 21st century. That is the mission, if you decide to take it on. I'm sure there might be times when it does seem like "Mission Impossible", but hey, Ethan Hunt always pulls it off in the end (cue theme song).

And remember, just like a good ole' catch line from a favorite movie, whenever you feel lost or overwhelmed or have forgotten your way, just say....

WOO DAT!

Made in the USA
Charleston, SC
21 September 2013